Praise for *With L*

Dawn Camp has gathered a bouque
common: They are mothers who love their daughters. The result is a fragrant collection of stories and letters that celebrate the mother-daughter dance—that relationship which brings with it every emotion imaginable and even a few that aren't. Read this book slowly. Savor the pages. Remember days past. Hope for days yet to come. And for all of it, give thanks.

—**John Blase,** author of *The Jubilee* and *Know When to Hold 'Em*

Dawn provides a window into the heart of what mother-daughter relationships are all about. She includes real-life stories that will make any reader laugh, cry, think, and remember. Full of heart-warming inspiration, this is a book that can be read over and over again.

—**Wendy Dunham,** award-winning author of *My Name Is River* and *Hope Girl*

She's done it again! In her fourth heartwarming story collection, *With Love, Mom,* gifted author Dawn Camp has gathered some of the finest Christian authors who share openly about the intimate dance of mother-daughter relationships. These transparent "pas de deux" stories pulse with delight, joy, doubts, challenges, humility, inspiration, and hope. Surprisingly, mothers often admit to learning intricate new dance steps from their daughters. But unquestionably each relationship flourishes with give and take, leading and listening. And always evident beneath each mother-daughter story beats the rhythm of God's love. This legacy book is a perfect gift for Mother's Day and any occasion. It will be repeatedly read and passed down through the generations from mother to daughter. I highly recommend it.

—**Lynn D. Morrissey,** author of *Love Letters to God* and *Treasures of a Woman's Heart*

A collection of wisdom and courage, heart and healing, love and honor... *With Love, Mom* is soul food for anyone who has ever called herself mom and for any girl who has ever loved and been loved by her mother.

—**Danielle Smith**, author of *Mom, Incorporated*

It often feels like mothers are sorted into boxes: stay-at-home, working, single, boy-mom, girl-mom, mom of multiples, and the like. But this collection of stories about motherhood does the complicated work of celebrating our differences while highlighting the similarities we all share. Rather than divide us up or pit us against each other, Dawn Camp has gathered all kinds of moms together to share their stories and their hearts. *With Love, Mom* will encourage anyone who has borne a child or been a child, anyone who has mothered or been mothered, anyone who longs to give and receive the love of a mom.

Mary Carver, coauthor of *Choose Joy*

Tears, laughter, and moments of deep-hearted connections were in each turn of the page in *With Love, Mom*. Beautiful and honest stories from women who help us see that motherhood is the most challenging job we will have. You will be encouraged as the love of Christ, through a mother's heart, transforms ordinary stories of life into extraordinary testimonies of love.

—**Diane Bailey**, author, speaker
and founder of the Consilium

With Love, Mom

DAWN CAMP

HARVEST HOUSE PUBLISHERS
EUGENE, OREGON

Cover by Connie Gabbert Design + Illustration

Cover photo by Dawn Camp

Published in association with William K. Jensen Literary Agency, 119 Bampton Court, Eugene, Oregon 97404.

WITH LOVE, MOM

Published by Harvest House Publishers
Eugene, Oregon 97408
www.harvesthousepublishers.com

ISBN 978-0-7369-7291-8 (pbk.)
ISBN 978-0-7369-7292-5 (eBook)

Printed in the United States of America

18 19 20 21 22 23 24 25 26 / BP-SK / 10 9 8 7 6 5 4 3 2 1

For my girls: Sabra, Chloe, Felicity, and Lily

WITH LOVE, MOM

Contents

PART 4: A MOTHER'S HOPE

PART 5: THE STRENGTH OF THE SINGLE MOTHER

PART 6: QUALITY TIME

PART 7: TEACHABLE MOMENTS

PART 8: MOTHER LOVE

PART 9: LEAVING A LEGACY

Foreword

Rachel Anne Ridge

Mothers and daughters.

These simple words hold a relationship that is filled with such beauty and complexity that it defies definition. Ask any woman what this relationship means and you'll likely get a long pause in response. Maybe you'll get an intake of breath and a run or two at putting words together. You'll probably get a far-off look as she tries to describe the love, the emotion, the frustration, the joy, the delight, the crazy, the tears, the uncertainties, the excitement, the fears, and the bond she shares with her daughter or her own mother. If a daughter happens to be next to a mother when the question is asked, you can bet the two will look at each other and search each other's faces for the right words to describe their bond. They will take in each other's eyes and expressions and feel a hundred emotions.

This is the mother-daughter relationship.

I love what Dawn has done with this collection of essays, letters, and chapters by mothers and daughters. As a mom of four girls, Dawn is intimately aware of the individuality of each daughter; how, in a sense, we are required to be a different kind of mom for each of our children. Every daughter has her own unique needs and gifts. As you mother girls, you revisit your relationship with your own mother and come to new understandings along the way. There is no "one size fits all" mothering style. What works for one daughter may not work for another.

Dawn understands all this. By finding a diversity of voices, she has gathered a treasure chest of wisdom, experience, and tenderness that beautifully reflects the many facets of raising daughters and appreciating our own mothers.

As you read the chapters in this book, you'll hear the voices of these women. Imagine being in a coffeehouse filled with the sounds of women sharing their mother-daughter stories—talking, and laughing, and probably shedding a tear or two. Pour yourself a cup of your favorite beverage and lean in. I encourage you to slow down and savor each story. Some of the voices you hear will lilt with a Southern twang; some shine from the plain-spoken Midwest, while others ring clear with the directness of the Northeast. Some of the voices carry the energy of youth, some the quiet of experience; all are filled with the kind of love only a mom can give her daughter, and the kind of love a daughter can give her mother.

I am captivated by the diversity of experiences, and yet no matter how different our stories are, there is a certain bond of sisterhood that comes with mothers and daughters. The ebbs and flows, the drama and pride, the uncertainties and doubts, the beauty—and sometimes the pain—that inevitably come with raising girls. Nothing can quite describe it, or even contain it.

My own two daughters are grown. They burst into my life as two little redheads, so full of life and energy and creativity. I wondered sometimes, well, lots of times, how on earth to raise these darling hooligans. They tested my patience, tried my mothering skills, drove me to my knees...and they delighted me to no end. They taught me, truly, how to love. My girls, Lauren and Meghan, now have daughters of their own. As I watch them raise their girls, I have a chance to see what I could not always see clearly when we were in the thick of figuring this "mother-daughter thing" out: I see just how precious this gift is. I see how beautiful it is.

If I could go back in time, here is what I wish I could tell the younger version of myself: Relax. Everything is going to be okay. If you're going to err, err on the side of grace—with yourself and with your daughters. Laugh as often as possible. Play together and make memories together. Gather with other moms. Stop comparing. Listen.

This book is an invitation to pull up a chair and listen to other moms and daughters. No matter where you are in your journey, you'll find encouragement, inspiration, and wisdom from this sisterhood of friends. I know you'll see something of yourself reflected here, or find a nugget that is just right for where you are today. Mothering girls is a beautiful gift, but it's not for the faint of heart. We need to rely on one another's strength and perspective, to help us navigate the choppy waters that inevitably come along the way. We need to remember those first moments of rapture with that new pink bundle, and we need the hope that one day that emotional teen can really be our best friend. We need to know that everything in between is part of a sacred journey.

That's what this book does.

I'm grateful for the many talents of Dawn Camp. With an artist's eye, she pulls beauty from the ordinary and creates spaces that feed the soul. This collection is just that kind of beautiful space. As you read you'll get to know her precious mom-heart that went into this book, and you'll know that you've found a sweet place to commune with women who remind us: the relationship between mothers and daughters is a precious gift to be cherished for a lifetime.

With love,
Rachel Anne Ridge
artist and author of
Flash, the Homeless Donkey Who Taught Me About Life, Faith and Second Chances

Acknowledgments

My girls—Gathering stories for this book and writing my own have deepened my appreciation for my mother and my daughters. I can't wait for granddaughters!

Bryan—You always support me, love. I couldn't do this without you.

Jacob, Hayden, Christian, and Clayton—Your sisters think this book proves I like them better. Maybe someday they will understand about mothers and sons.

My contributors—Thank you for trusting me with your sweet words and photos.

My church family—Your love and your prayers recharge me. You're my best friends.

Ruth Samsel, my agent—If I'm your favorite Southern belle, you're my favorite Yankee. Thank you for all you do for me.

Kathleen Kerr at Harvest House—It has been so much fun working with you. You rock.

Shelby Zacharias at Harvest House—You have lightened my load immeasurably by handling details and letting me focus on the work. Bless you!

My Lord, Jesus Christ—Every blessing I owe to You. Thank You for continued opportunities to praise Your name.

Introduction

I was one of two girls, as was my mother, so I assumed my first child would be a daughter. It's what I knew. One day in the middle of my first pregnancy I actually exclaimed, "Wait! What if it's a boy?" It took weeks for the idea to occur to me. My mother-in-law, who gave birth to three boys with a husband who was one of three boys, said, "You'll have a boy. The Camps have boys." And I, with the confidence and inexperience of youth, declared I had a 50/50 chance either way (but secretly I knew I'd have a girl, because *my* family had girls).

It was the first of many times my instincts would prove wrong along the journey of motherhood. I gave birth to not one, not two, but three boys before the mild December day when a girl joined our clan. Ultimately my husband and I would produce an even mix of boys and girls—four of each—but we were parents for ten years before we brought home a baby swaddled in pink.

Although initially I couldn't imagine having sons, I had started to wonder if we would ever have daughters. I grew up playing softball and was a bit of a tomboy; I loved sitting in the bleachers, watching and keeping score at my sons' baseball games. Surely God wouldn't think I didn't need a girl since I was a good boy mom? I can French braid hair, for goodness' sake! Such were the crazy thoughts that filled my head in the years before our first daughter was born. When the ultrasound technician declared our fourth child a girl, I asked, "Would you stake your professional reputation on it?" The answer was yes. I later told my husband I was 95 percent certain we were having another boy. He replied, "I was 99 percent."

My first daughter and I share the same middle name, a gift from my daddy in honor of the Dallas Cowboys' star quarterback at the time of my birth, Don Meredith. I never imagined we'd have three more girls or I might have saved it for another daughter's first name. A fellow boy-mom-who-eventually-had-a-girl told me having a daughter didn't feel different until around the first birthday, but for me everything was different from day one. I was different too.

My four girls are each unique. It's a marvel how the same house and the same parents can produce such different results! And just as we change over the course of our lives, our daughters do too. The independent child who pushes you away may someday become a hugger who whispers, "I love you." A mother's relationship with her daughter may ebb and flow throughout the years, but a mother's love is constant.

Parenting girls is different for a mother than a father. My mother once told me in her eyes my boys could do no wrong, but she could see right through my girls. She then said that my dad didn't see how my husband could get upset with our daughters over anything. That mother-son and father-daughter thing is *real* and also multigenerational.

A mother understands a daughter in ways her husband never can. We remember somersaulting across the lawn, teenage hormones, learning to apply makeup, our first broken heart. The force of our will cannot keep our daughters from repeating our mistakes, and in the moments when they do, it's hard to recognize that these lessons shape them into the women they'll become, the same way they shaped us. Motherhood can deepen our well of empathy; it's a wise mother whose lips speak comfort rather than "I told you so."

It's been a delight to compile this treasury of stories from mothers to their daughters and daughters to their mothers (and grandmothers). When possible, we've included pictures of the women and girls that each story represents. You'll find tales of daughters from newborn to adult; from toddlers to twins to teens; from birth stories to the blessing of adoption; and the courage of the single mother: all accounts of our hopes and our fears for our daughters, and what it means both to bestow and to receive a legacy. I hope they bless you and you see your story reflected in these pages.

Blessings,
Dawn

Part 1

Words of Affirmation

Death and life are in the power of the tongue.

PROVERBS 18:21

1

She Says I'm Her Best Friend

Dawn Camp

It took 19 years of parenthood and seven other children before I gave birth to the one I call my mini-me. She arrived the year after my mother passed away, and we moved when she was six weeks old. If that wasn't stressful enough, we owned two houses for seven months (we bought one before the other sold—never again!). During those long, hard months when I missed my mother fiercely and worried we would lose both homes, this tiny daughter became my lifeline. In the midst of worry and depression, I drew strength and comfort from her touch; caring for an infant, so totally dependent on me, brought meaning and purpose to difficult days.

Now she is 12 years old, and while my Lily has the crowd-pleasing, outgoing personality stereotypical of the baby in a family, she also shares many classic characteristics of a firstborn, like me. Sometimes exactly like me. She can be stubborn and illogical, but she's not afraid to speak her mind and tell her brothers and sisters the way things should be done. Her instincts are remarkably good (maybe because she pays attention to the way *I* want things to be done), which makes her instructions even less popular. Who wants to be told what to do by their little sister? Especially if she's right?

She's always been precocious. I'll never forget the day she learned to ride a bike without training wheels. No one taught her—she just asked one of the kids to pick her up and put her on the seat and away she went! At barely four years old her feet didn't touch the ground, but that didn't stop my Lily. Very little stops my Lily.

Occasionally, however, I'm reminded that my big, brave daughter is really just a little girl. This spring a friend asked Lily to join her family for nine days at her grandmother's house on the beach. Our other kids were jealous. We were all jealous. But from almost the moment she passed beyond the distance where going to get her might have been an option, Lily was struck with a powerful case of homesickness.

She contacted me constantly and in every possible way: text, phone call, Skype, FaceTime, Instagram chat. She would have sent smoke signals if she knew how.

Mommy, I miss you.

I'm homesick.

I miss you, Mommy.

The same words, over and over, again and again, day after day. I'm not sure which of us was more miserable. Her friend's mother called and texted me too. It was hard for her to watch, but thankfully Lily was with good people who loved her.

She left on Sunday, and I dropped a card in the mail Monday morning. I told her to check the mailbox each day; the anticipation seemed to do her good. She called on Thursday when it arrived, a hint of happiness in her voice. Lily and I talked as I drove my fifteen-year-old son home from track practice, her voice transmitting clearly through my car's speakers.

"I thought Ryan and Riley were my best friends...but, Mommy, you're my best friend."

My son and I looked at each other, identical raised eyebrows and looks of wonderment on our faces, and it was clear I was not the only one who believed no sweeter words had been spoken. Later we ordered Lily her favorite board game with two-day shipping, since she wouldn't be home for another five days. It provided the suspense of a surprise before it arrived and hours of play and distraction afterward, and it seemed to spark a turning point: she enjoyed her final days at the beach.

It was in the months before this trip when I'd started to worry about our final years of parenting children at home. Over a 19-year period we'd added one child at a time until we reached eight, and then almost immediately they began to stretch their wings and leave the nest. Our oldest left for college when Lily was only two months old. Would she think her last years here were too quiet when she was the only child left at home? Would she grow tired of just us?

Lily has no idea what a gift her simple words were to me that day when she told me I was her best friend, the balm they were to my heart. I don't know what the years ahead will hold as she bursts into her teens and I ease further into my fifties. Experience tells me to expect a mixture of highs and lows, like forecasting the weather. But I know that on a warm, spring day, not too long ago, she declared me her best friend and I embraced it with my very soul.

Someday I may read her this story, to remind us both.

A mother is a daughter's first best friend.

AUTHOR UNKNOWN

2

Did You See Me?

Teri Lynne Underwood

From the edge of the stage I watched, holding my breath as the music began. I watched the tiny ballet-slippered feet tap and turn, uncertain but determined. She slipped a quick glance my direction and I smiled and gave the thumbs-up. And then, in the blink of an eye, the dance was done and my tiny dancer was wrapped up in my arms asking if I saw that she didn't forget a single part of her very first recital dance.

"I saw you, baby! I saw every second. And it was beautiful. You were great! I'm so proud."

She bounced her way off with her other tiny dancer friends, all of them equally excited and enthusiastic.

Since that long-ago day of itty-bitty ballet shoes, I've watched countless other recitals and performances. And every time her dance is complete, the same question: "Did you see me, Mom?"

"Yes, my sweet girl, I saw you. You were great! I'm so proud."

She's worn tiny little ballet shoes, loud black tap shoes, toe shoes tied up with ribbons, and most every other kind of dance shoe there is. We've got piles of tights and leotards, leg warmers and wraps. Then she traded in her dance shoes and tights for cheerleading shoes and pom-poms.

I sat in the stands, cheering with her and for her. And after every game, the question, "Did you see me, Mom?"

"Yes, my sweet girl, I saw you. You were great! I'm so proud."

Her cheerleading days are now over. She'll all too soon don her high heels and cap and gown and I'll be sitting there, watching just like I always have, as she moves from one season of life into the next.

She looked at me recently, eyes full of tears, and said, "I miss you." Teary-eyed myself, I told her I felt the same. All those years of dance and cheer had given us hours of time together. But chemistry study groups and her first job don't require a mom's presence. She drives herself wherever she needs to go.

I've long felt the awareness of the shift in our relationship. Knowing she felt the same was equal parts reassuring and heartbreaking.

We planned a mother-daughter day out and decided we'd go shoe shopping. Laughing as we tried on shoes we'd never buy and finally settling on a pair for each of us, she grabbed my hand and said, "Mom, thank you. For always being here and always seeing me."

I fought back the tears as I said, "Oh, beautiful girl, I will always see you. And I will always believe in you. And I will always be so proud of you."

And I will.

Never lose an opportunity
of seeing anything that is beautiful;
for beauty is God's handwriting—
a wayside sacrament.
Welcome it in every fair face,
in every fair sky, in every fair flower,
and thank God for it as a cup of blessing.

RALPH WALDO EMERSON

3

Let Her Be

Rachel Macy Stafford

When my daughter Avery was six years old, I found her surveying herself in front of the mirror. Although I'd come into her room to comment on her hair and outfit, as I typically did when she was getting dressed, that day was different. I peered through the slightly open door and quietly watched.

Initially, my eyes rested on the too-snug waistband of her favorite shorts and the uncombed clump of hair sticking from the back of her head—but then God showed me what I most needed to see.

Reflected in the mirror before her was pure joy. Pure contentment. Pure peace all at the sight of her six-year-old self.

Then she twirled in front of that mirror, actually twirled. Upon her second rotation, she saw me at the door wiping tears from my eyes. She gave me a glorious smile—a smile that said, "I feel beautiful, Mama."

That's when a divinely protective voice inside me whispered, "Let her be."

Let her be.

For the first time in my life, I would not disturb my child's inner contentment under the guise of making a "good impression."

Besides, who was I to say what her *best impression* was anyway? She believed she looked beautiful and that was enough.

It suddenly dawned on me that unlike her blue eyes and freckles, she did not have to inherit my issues and insecurities. I could decide right then and there I would *not* pass my issues to her. Plus, why would I want to?

Why would I want her to stand in front of the mirror for the rest of her life seeing *too much* and *not enough* when she could see *just right*?

Why would I want her to go through life wondering what other people thought of her when she was quite happy with *who she was*?

Since that defining moment five years ago, I've clung to God's freeing words, *let her be,* as Avery and her sister have grown. As my daughters make decisions regarding their physical appearance and their academic studies, as they complete household duties and interact with peers, as they make eating choices and life decisions, I am there to support and encourage, but I no longer dictate, critique, or control.

Letting them be is not easy, but I lived for over thirty years with the critical voice of *not enough*. Basing my worth on superficial measures of success left me sad and empty, and I don't want that for my daughters. As I've established meaningful measures of success, I feel God's loving assurance healing decades of damage and filling the emptiness in my soul. By accepting God's unconditional love and grace for myself, I've been able to offer it to my children.

I am prepared to watch them soar and stumble as they live their truths in the light of self-love and acceptance rather than constantly second-guessing themselves and their decisions.

Perhaps this approach sounds inviting to you, but you're not sure where to start.

It starts with being kind to yourself about your issues and insecurities. They aren't going to disappear overnight, but awareness and compassion are empowering and life-altering.

It starts with repeating the mantra "only love today" when the inner bully gets loud in your head and starts coming out of your mouth.

It starts with remembering to look through your children's eyes before you evaluate. Perhaps where you see room for improvement, they see *just right*.

It starts with remembering your loved ones have teachers, bosses, coaches, and instructors who are there to offer critiques and improvements. That leaves you to listen, love, and support.

It starts with asking yourself: Is this suggestion I'm about to give going to sound like help or judgment? Perhaps you don't need to say anything at all. Chances are, they're doing the best they can, just like you.

It starts when we decide to stop worrying about how our children's appearance and achievements reflect on us and start focusing on how our unconditional love reflects on them.

Our issue is not their issue—at least, it doesn't have to be.

Let's step back and give them plenty of room to twirl.

We just never know who they might become if we let them be.

If you see something beautiful in someone, speak it.

RUTHIE LINDSEY

4

The Perfect Mother

Robin Dance

I'm anchored to a familiar perch, a red stool at our kitchen bar. It's one of my favorite writing spots, overlooking a squirrel's playground every day and a bunny sanctuary on my luckiest days.

She rounds the kitchen corner in a burst of morning energy, her bare face and ponytail reminding me of days gone by, when she was seven or eight—not 18 going on 19. Forty-five minutes earlier I had slipped beside her in bed.

—

"Sorry I'm waking you up later than you asked," I whispered, and she croaked an unintelligible reply and turned from her side to her stomach. It was an invitation as far as I was concerned.

I combed my fingers through her hair. Once silky golden, her curls had matured into coarse, dirty-blonde tangles. Still beautiful, just different. She never uses a brush because that would make her hair "big"; she has no regard for Texas or the '80s.

I follow the strands down her neck and brush them to the side, rubbing her back. "I remember when my hand covered your entire back," and she responds with a muffled chuckle. "Scratch with your fingernails," she begs. Up and down, back and forth, I carve memory into this moment.

—

With Bible and notebook in hand, she's headed outside for what she calls her "Jesus time." Her discipline and devotion and love for God are so pure, and I admire that in her. I covet it.

She lays her things on the counter, deciding to toast an English muffin first. Out of the blue she declares, "I'm so thankful God gave me the perfect mother."

She doesn't play fair—this I've long known—and I wasn't prepared for her pronouncement. Tears from nowhere fill my eyes and I blurt, "Don't leave me!" then instantly, "No, you need to leave me!" and she understands I'm talking about college.

I know it must sound like I'm a basket case at times, or maybe a helicopter parent, but really, I'm fine. I do feel the depth and ache of my first child leaving home, true, but it is what we've always desired for our children: healthy independence. I'd be much sadder if she were clinging to us and dreading this wonderful season of life.

She knows how to fix this quickly.

"I mean, you aren't too perfect, the annoying kind, but what kind of mom would still take the time to lie down with me and play with my hair and scratch my back?"

Her English muffin now slathered in strawberry jam, she picks up her books and heads out the door, leaving me buried under a pile of memories and dreams and a single prayer. No, a praise to God—

Thank You for giving me the perfect daughter.

I guess that makes us even.

I will bless the LORD at all times: his praise shall continually be in my mouth.

PSALM 34:1

5

Dear Daughter of Mine

Anna Rendell

Dear Daughter of mine,

Right now I'm pregnant with your coming sibling. I still have pounds leftover from housing you and your big brother. My weeks-old pedicure is all kinds of chipped, and in this summer humidity my frizz-prone hair will not hold a curl or straighten. I feel less than every other woman on the Internet and in the grocery store and at the library. I do not feel beautiful. I feel like a human house.

But your daddy. You see the way he takes my hand, holds me close, and tells me I'm beautiful. And when he says that, dear girl, he's talking about much more than smooth skin and straightened hair.

He's taught your brother to see the beauty in Mommy, and in you, and every day they tell us how beautiful we are—inside and out. You are growing up held in love by a family who believes in the power of beauty, of that which glows from the inside of our hearts and home and lights up a face and a neighborhood.

Even when I may feel less than, with the love of these boys I remember truth. With their love put into action, I can feel myself soften to actually believe it. To believe I'm beautiful even when I feel anything but.

See, my girl, the size of our clothes cannot tell us how pretty we are. No blemish on our face or dark circles under our eyes can take away from our beauty. The out-of-control story our hair tells is not the whole truth. And while makeup can cover a multitude of late nights and crack-of-dawn mornings, it can't define our lovely. You sit with me, watching as I apply that makeup, asking for just a little blush or lip gloss. When you're older I'll teach you how to properly use makeup, and to paint your nails, and to carefully choose the clothes that make us feel our best. It's okay to embrace our femininity and love it...but it's also important to know that these things are just icing.

You are not responsible for your beauty, sweetness. God has already planted every bit of it, and the loveliest things about you are unchangeable. Your deep and wide loving heart that causes you to consistently put others first. You shine with kindness as you grab an extra snack for your big brother, care gently for your friends, and share whatever books or treat or crayons you're holding in your dimpled hands. The way you love to tenderly pet our dear old Golden Retriever. Your head of soft, brown curls that match the sparkle in your chocolate-brown eyes. The way you tilt your head and grin knowingly when you want to do something from the no-no list. The forever-bronzed color of your skin, inherited from your daddy. The way you snuggle into our necks and shoulders, knowing that's your very own spot where you will always fit. When you reach your arms up to be carried in love, trusting the ones who bend to pick you up and carry you on.

It's these things and more that make you my gorgeous girl. I will always see and cherish each one of these qualities in you, even—maybe more so—on the days when you cannot. I will remind you that you were created in beauty, with care and specific purpose by the One who calls us good. I will dry your tears and gently remind you that it's not our outsides that make us lovely. I will teach you as I try to model with my own living that while you can't control your beauty, you can own it. Your daddy and I see your beauty, the inside kind. We all see it in you, love, and give thanks to the One who pieced you together by His mighty hand.

Favour is deceitful, and beauty is vain:
but a woman that feareth the
Lord, she shall be praised.

PROVERBS 31:30

6

Mother's Melody

Lynn D. Morrissey

For my beloved mother, Fern, with all my love

She sang life to me unconditionally
as I grew in her secret cocoon
and bloomed to completion.

She sang contentment.
Nesting me at her breast,
we rocked and rocked in quilted quiet.
My curls rose and fell with her breath.

She sang ivory lullabies,
rock-a-bye babies, hush-a-byes,
by yon bonnie banks and farmers' dells.
The tunes soared and swelled 'til I was compelled to sing
a ring around her rosy beauty.

She sang comfort on rain-throated days
and brought tea and toast.
I floated in her blue-quilt sea,
gently bedded.

She sang love to me sacrificially.
I was in her.
Now she's in me.
I am my mother's melody.

I have calmed and quieted myself,
I am like a weaned child with its mother;
like a weaned child I am content.

PSALM 131:2 NIV

Part 2

Perfectly Imperfect

Imperfections are not inadequacies; they are reminders that we're all in this together.

BRENÉ BROWN

7

A Relationship Worth Fighting For

Elizabeth Maxon

Her hair was a tousled mess on the top of her head. She wore only the pink-and-white-striped undies she slept in and the insulin pump connected to her hip. With her thumb she pressed the button through the Hello Kitty pouch to make the pump screen light up. She announced dramatically, in a loud whisper, "My pump says it's 7:05! How is that even possible? It's still dark outside!"

A grin spread across her face as I explained it was, in fact, true, and the clouds had covered the morning sun. She danced lightly on tiptoe and said something about how she should have known because her tummy was hungry for breakfast.

As she skipped back down the hallway to find some clothes, I sat on the couch feeling like I had just been the audience for a highly acclaimed Broadway performance. I was delighted by her. If that show had started while I was still blurry-eyed in bed, my response probably would have been totally different. Thankfully, on that particular day I had resisted the snooze button and dragged myself out of bed early, just as I intend to do every day. It's my chance to get my head and my heart right before they need me. It's the difference in my feeling enchanted versus exasperated with her, with them, my little people.

Barely a minute passed before she returned in her purple silk Rapunzel gown with her sewing kit in hand. Ready to begin.

If I'm not ready to begin before she's ready to begin, the day always turns out differently. Within seconds of her eyes opening, her mouth opens too. And then it rarely closes. Between eating and talking, she is a busy girl. Her brother is slower to start. Quiet and observant at times. Sometimes it seems that 99.9 percent of Lucy's waking hours are filled with words.

Spoken.

Sung.

Occasionally screamed.

She completely fills the space around her.

Light does that—reaches out into all the emptiness offering color and life.

—

I told the lady, "Her name is Lucy. It means light."

Just as the wedding ceremony of some family friends had concluded, someone sitting behind us had tapped me on the shoulder and asked with a smile, "Is that your daughter?"

I nodded.

"She is beautiful."

I felt the burn of tears surfacing in the corners of my eyes.

"Thank you," I said with a smile.

"I was just watching the way she sat with you, held your hands, and the way her face lights up when she talks to you."

That's when I told her Lucy's name and what it means. In that moment the tear was set free down my cheek. The woman's eyes glistened too as her smile widened. At the time I couldn't have explained why a two-minute interaction with a stranger was so significant to me—so holy. I'm still not sure, but here's my suspicion.

This child is not easy.

Others have witnessed much different scenes—both of us looking more ugly than beautiful amidst tears and tantrums. There were days when I was literally fighting for a relationship with her. There has been tension between us. I have looked at her and seen myself as a failure, and yet continued to love her fiercely. There is no lukewarm love for a child like that. She demands more. She also offers more.

Although the woman's words said something else, their meaning told me this: *I see the two of you together, and it is beautiful. There is something in the way you relate to each other that is lovely to witness. It is something noticeable, something special. I see love there.*

It was the sweet feeling of a hard-fought victory I felt in that moment.

The child who rarely said, "I love you" to me the first four years of her life.

The child who shot me looks of anger more than looks of love.

That same child now climbs up on my lap during a movie (or a wedding ceremony) and weaves her fingers into mine and gets as close to me as she possibly can and whispers softly, "I love you, Mama."

That same child at bedtime will ask for more hugs and more kisses and more snuggle time in the bed. She will shout as I pull her door closed, "I love you more than chocolate!"

Maybe you have a tough kid too. Maybe you have some other tough relationship. Maybe you feel like there is an impenetrable wall between you and someone you desperately want to love well. Maybe it feels all wrong. Maybe the relationship isn't at all what you imagined it would be.

Listen.

Don't give up.

I can't tell you when and I can't tell you how, but if God gives you someone difficult to love, somehow and some way love will penetrate the wall—maybe even dissolve it to the ground. The past seven years I have spent learning how to love my daughter well—with His love, not my own. I have prayed grace over all the times I've messed up. It has been a battle, emotionally and spiritually.

Daily I choose not to fight *with* her, but to fight *for* her. And I never give up. That has made all the difference. That kind of fighting has led to victory.

So keep fighting the good fight, friends. I know it's not easy. I know sometimes you lose a battle, but pick yourself back up and remember—victory is coming, and the war is already won.

Perseverance, secret of all triumphs.

VICTOR HUGO

8
A Love Letter for a Second-Born Child

Jennifer Dukes Lee

Dear Daughter,

I loved you instantly, of course.

It was the second time in my life that a delivery-room nurse had placed a wrinkled newborn girl in my arms.

When my lips brushed across your cheek, I knew it would be a cinch to love you as much as I loved your big sister. But I knew I'd need to love you differently.

I was smitten. And I was terrified—not of what *you'd* be like, but what *I'd* be like as your mother. What if I made comparisons? And what if my sloppy parenting ruined you for life?

Sure, I loved you instantly. But what if I didn't love you *right*?

My dog-eared pregnancy books didn't yield answers. The right answers would need to be lived over the rugged terrain of years.

Your older sister was the echo of my soul, my own mini-me. Mothering her has always felt like parenting an updated version of myself. But you, dear daughter? You were a mystery. Discipline techniques that worked on your sister would throw you into a red-faced toddler rage. You zigged when I zagged. You wanted to color outside the lines—and on the walls. We now know your inner artist was simply trying to find a way to bust loose.

My worst fear? That I would accidentally bust up what God created while trying to recreate you in my own image.

Your sister is the classic firstborn—high-achieving, organized, and responsible. She has a color-coordinated closet, shiny trophies, and clever stories to keep us entertained at the supper table.

I knew enough about birth order to know that you might grow up feeling like you were living in someone's shadow. And your big sister has always cast a very big shadow.

Everybody talked about what a "perfect baby" your sister was. She was happy and precocious and whip-smart. You're ten years old now, and you found out a long time ago that your 13-year-old sister is the life of the party and the top of the Honor Roll.

Your sister holds microphones confidently in front of big audiences, sharing about our family's love for Haiti. You sit beside me watching her, and we hold hands. I squeeze your hand and press my forehead against yours, because I want you to know that I am as proud of you as I am of her. Your love for Haiti is no less fiery than hers. You have been on the same trips, and you do some amazing things too. You simply don't feel as comfortable telling a big crowd of people about it. But I've never once seen you jealous about all of that.

At night, by the light of your lamp, I pray with you. I tell God out loud how proud I am of you—and how awesome you are. (I don't typically speak for God, but I think it's safe to say that He agrees with me.)

Daughter, have I told you lately how talented and beautiful and smart and funny and compassionate you are?

For heaven's sake, what's not to love? You wear lobsters on your shirt, and you teach me to make emoji cookies. Kid, you crack me up.

You are your very own *you*. God forbid that I would put you in a box neatly drawn by your birth order, some personality test, some expectation that you're extraverted or introverted or whatever-verted. You are, simply, you. Beautiful, one-of-a-kind you.

You don't belong in a box with tight boundaries. You belong to a God of boundless grace.

You can trust God with your story because He is the one who wrote it. You don't have to live up to someone else's expectations—including what your own mother might mistakenly project on you.

May God forgive me if I ever cause you to operate out of fear. May you only operate out of your enough-ness.

Dear child, I watch with deep admiration how you are blooming into your own brand of awesome. I watch and I learn from you.

Every spring I see how you run for the lilacs when they begin to bloom. You always press your whole self into the scent of spring.

I envy you in those moments, how you lose yourself in a scrubby old bush in our backyard. I used to do that when I was your age. So in a way, you remind me of me—the me I want to be again, the me that gets lost in the inglorious nature of maturity.

Keep up with your you-ness, dear child. It's beautiful. Color outside the lines. Pray your quiet prayers. Keep rejecting fear. Don't stop trusting God with your story. Stay spontaneous. Don't let maturity rob you of your zippiness.

Wear lobsters on your shirt forever-and-ever-amen. Remember you're preapproved. And keep reminding me too, okay?

And always, always, dear girl, run for the lilacs.

I love you.
Mom

Always be a first-rate version of yourself instead of a second-rate version of somebody else.

JUDY GARLAND

9

A Song for You

Christie Purifoy

This is a familiar story. I am sure you have a version of your own.

It's a story of how one song can snag and hold a memory that might otherwise have been lost. It's a story of how every time that one song plays, you are transported. This is less like remembering and more like time travel.

Mine is a summer story. The experts said it was the coolest Chicago summer in a decade. I've never liked hot weather, and that summer I was heavy with an unborn girl. The lake breezes lifting the curtains in our bedroom seemed to whisper certain promises: "The empty days are over, the future is full and bright."

I had emerged from the long, dark winter of infertility. I'd survived a spring of euphoria and illness. Now I was cocooned in the mellow hormones of the third trimester. I'm sure it wasn't all sweet dreaminess. I suppose there were cloudy nights, but that's not how I remember it. I remember long walks with my husband as the sun sank in a puddle of sherbet colors. I remember long drives along the lakeshore when moonlight swam on the water.

That summer we could hardly turn on the radio without hearing the song "Yellow" by Coldplay. It was a song about the stars, and it was a song about love, and hope, and longing. Perhaps it only happened once, but when I think of those months this is what I remember: a nighttime drive down the length of Chicago's lakefront, city lights overhead like glittery stars, windows rolled down, a long-desired baby girl filling me up, and "Yellow" playing just for us on the radio.

That song and my daughter: they've been tangled up in my mind ever since.

Which is a gift.

Now when I hear that song, I am taken right back to a place and a feeling it's important I never forget. I hear the song, and I remember how she and I were once held, still and steady, by a love that belonged to us yet was so much bigger than us. I hear the song, and I remember my child of promise and possibility.

It can be difficult, and often impossible, to hold on to those feelings through sleepless nights, temper tantrums, meltdowns over melted ice cream and missing homework, and years of hormonal grumpiness (hers and mine). It can be hard to hold on to hope in the midst of all the ordinary awfulness of our ordinary days.

But the ordinary awful is a distraction. It is not the real thing. It doesn't tell us who we really are. It tries to obscure the truth of who our child really is. My daughter is a teenager now, and more and more I am convinced that good mothering is learning to coast through the awfulness without losing my grip on the truth.

And the truth is this: life is magical, motherhood is an indescribably good gift, and my daughter (yours too) is more precious and beautiful than even the nighttime sky.

Daughter, you are a bright star, a shining, yellow moon, and I love you.

Every heart sings a song, incomplete,
until another heart whispers back.

ANONYMOUS

10

Mommy, Did You Choose Your Job?

Danielle Smith

"Mommy, did you choose your job?" my small girl asked curiously.

A smile snuck across my face as I straightened my spine and took a deep breath, imagining the beauty of the mother-daughter conversation that was to come. The light in my eyes must have reflected my enthusiasm. She had *noticed* that I was choosing to do a job I love every day.

"Yes, I most certainly *did* choose my job," I replied with more than a little pride, anticipating the slew of "How, why, and can I do it too?" that was certain to follow.

She tilted her head, her ringlets bobbing with the movement, her deep chocolate eyes gazing steadily at me. And then she spoke again.

"Then why in the world would you ever choose a job that takes you away from me so much?"

The air disappeared from the room. I like to joke to other mothers when I tell this story that I needed to take a moment to remove the guilt-shaped knife from my back, but the reality is, my small girl missed me when I was gone. And she blamed me for being the one to pull away.

Yes, I travel. I had just returned from a six-week book tour, coming home only a few days at a time. This wasn't the norm, but as a child, she didn't know if we were settling into a new normal.

Clearly she deserved an answer.

I pulled her into my lap and tipped that sweet, freckled face upward until our eyes met.

And then I told her a story.

"Punky, during an interview just last week when I was on book tour, I was asked what I want my kids to say about me at the end of the day. You know what I want you to say when you are all grown up? *My mom did both.* She was a present mother—she was there *most* nights to tuck us in and say prayers, to make dinner, to be here when we got home from school. She was at nearly every baseball, softball, and basketball game, but she never stopped being who *she* wanted to be when she grew up. You see, little one, I want you to see the time I am here with you and to see me doing the work that I love…and know that someday you can do the same."

I could see her tiny wheels turning.

I could see a calm coming over her.

I could see her picturing a bigger version of herself doing *both*.

The smile and the hug that followed assured me that even though I've chosen a job that "takes me away" sometimes, it is okay for my small girl to miss me. It is okay for her to see the imbalance in motherhood and love and work and to know that the puzzle can still fit together beautifully.

And it is definitely okay for me to miss her right back when I'm in the midst of doing this crazy, amazing job I chose.

It takes courage to grow up and
become who you really are.

E.E. CUMMINGS

11

Sweet Sixteen

Denise J. Hughes

The glass shatters. I hear the clanging of a crowbar as the paramedic lets it fall to the ground. He then reaches through the broken window and holds my head still while another paramedic wraps a brace around my neck. Their silence worries me, and I can't turn my head to see if my mom is okay. But I notice the clock on the dashboard, blinking the time.

The next thing I know I'm lying on the ground with only a thin, wooden board separating me from the gravel. Somebody tapes my forehead to the stretcher as the hail continues to pound my face. I want to see what's happening, but my only defense against the angry sky is to close my eyes.

The sound of raining ice-rocks drowns a nearby siren as the paramedic asks me dumb questions.

"What is your name?"

Denise.

"How are old you?"

Sixteen.

"When is your birthday?"

Today.

He pauses long enough for me to ask, "Is my mom okay?" But he evades my question and says we're being transported to the nearest hospital, which is an hour away. The two men carry me on the stretcher to the waiting ambulance.

Forced to stare at the ceiling of the ambulance, I hear my mom answering similar questions. She sounds okay, but the concern in her voice troubles me. A flurry of detached voices surrounds us. Nobody will explain what is happening, and the drive takes more than an hour. Fear consumes me more than the pain.

My sixteenth birthday.

We were supposed to spend the day shopping. Just Mom and me. But a sudden hailstorm froze the highway, causing someone to crash into us from behind. Now it's a trip to the hospital instead of the mall.

After X-rays and an examination, we're released with some ugly bruises and Goliath-size bandages. But we're thankful nothing more serious was damaged or broken. Except Mom's car was totaled. And I'm secretly glad I wasn't driving. If I had crashed Mom's car on the first day of getting my driver's license, I'd never hear the end of it. But she didn't want me driving on the freeway for a while yet. I tried to protest, and may have even rolled my eyes because of her obvious overprotectiveness, but now I'm thankful for it.

Decades later, this day comes to mind because I'm now planning my own daughter's sixteenth birthday. She'll remember it forever. And I want it to be fun. Memorable. In a good way.

Our culture makes a big deal out of "Sweet Sixteen," but that's not why it's important to me. Nor am I trying to redeem my own disastrous sixteenth birthday. The truth is, I lie awake at night because I can almost hear a clock ticking. From somewhere deep inside, my pulse quickens and I can't escape it. I started hearing this inner clock when my daughter turned nine. Her ninth birthday marked a sort of "halfway point" for me.

Halfway to 18.

Halfway to college.

Halfway to moving away.

Tick, tock.

The clock is moving too fast, and I can't slow it down. There is so much I want to do for her—and with her—before she graduates. Places I'd like to see together. Mission trips I'd like to take together. Talks I'd like to have together. There is so much I want us to share before time runs out. And yet there are other things I wish I could erase from time. Things I wish I would have done differently. Things I wish I would have said differently.

But I do know this: none of us moms ever do this motherhood thing perfectly. Oh, we may try, only to realize how much we need God's grace just to get through the day. And that's what I'm most thankful for: that when I fail, God's grace is sufficient to make up the difference. No matter what I do, God's love will always reach further and deeper than my love ever could.

Yes, the clock is ticking. Much too fast. Sixteen birthdays already. Sixteen Mother's Days too. And only two more before she leaves for college. I know I cannot do all that I would like to do. There probably won't be a trip to London or a weekend in Paris before she graduates. But there can be other things. Perhaps more important things. Intentional conversations. Intentional memories.

A few days after my sixteenth birthday, my mom set a vase of 16 pink roses on our dining room table. From the fridge, she pulled a cake out of a baker's box and we sat together. She apologized that my sixteenth birthday wasn't the special shopping day it was supposed to be, with just us. But it didn't matter. In that moment all that mattered was that we were there.

That's the best gift we can ever give. We can give of ourselves. Our time. And our presence.

Teach us to number our days, that we
may apply our hearts unto wisdom.

PSALM 90:12

Part 3

Learning from Our Mother and Our Daughters

The attitude you have as a parent is what your kids will learn from more than what you tell them. They don't remember what you try to teach them. They remember what you are.

JIM HENSON

12

The Day She Taught Me About Forgiveness

Kayla Aimee

When the morning light was just peeking over the tops of the trees, my four-year-old daughter, Scarlette, shuffled into my room, all ruffled hair and clutching her blanket. She climbed up into my bed, put her little hands on my cheeks, and said very seriously, "Mommy, why does your face look like that?"

I had not gotten much sleep the night before, thanks to neighbors who think the recent legality of fireworks in Georgia means that they should shoot them off all night long while blaring old-school Will Smith records at alarming volumes. I mean, I like to "Get Jiggy with It" because it reminds me of my high school class doing a choreographed dance to that song during our yearly Class Games. It's just that I like to do it at appropriate times during the day—like, say, three o'clock in the afternoon. Not three o'clock in the morning. Do you know what I like to do at three o'clock in the morning? Sleep. I like to sleep.

According to Scarlette, having my sleep so disturbed had apparently made my face look "smooshy, kinda like a tomato." That is always a good motivation for waking up in the morning, I find. Then she said to me, "Mommy. I weally need to tell you somefing. I forgive you."

And I was all, "Oh, thank you, Scarlette. Um…what for, exactly?"

And she said, "For being my mommy!"

"Oh," I replied. "Well, okay. Thank you. Maybe you could tell me what you think forgiveness means, though, just real quick."

"*Mommy*," she said slowly. Clearly she was explaining this concept to someone who really needed to grasp it. "Forgiveness is when you are *loving* somebody. Dat is what God says it means, so I just telling you I forgive you *so much*!"

I feel like somehow this slight mix-up is still completely doctrinally sound.

Maybe she has the definition wrong, but the context is for sure and certain: forgiveness is born from love. I birthed it alongside of her as she entered this world, this new capacity for love that is more than I can hold. It reminds me of the Maker's, deep and wide and ever alongside us, the way it continuously unfolds to cover everything. It is motherhood that opened me up to this, that showed me how love unending flows in to fill the gaps. Where I used to grip tightly to a grudge, I now find myself softening. I'm quicker to forgive because she is right; forgiveness is loving somebody.

The only tiny issue is the part about how she keeps flinging her arms around me in public, like at the grocery store, and loudly declaring, "I forgive you, Mommy!" Which isn't at all awkward and definitely doesn't generate some questioning looks being thrown in my direction.

Although to be fair, they *could* just be thinking to themselves, *That woman needs a good night's sleep. She looks all smooshy, like a tomato.*

Be ye kind one to another, tenderhearted,
forgiving one another, even as God for
Christ's sake hath forgiven you.

EPHESIANS 4:32

13

Stay Weird: A Letter to My Daughter

Mary Carver

Last summer Annalyn rediscovered a pair of lab goggles that we'd used for a science experiment a couple years ago. At first she used them to protect her eyes in the shower, but quickly she moved on to wearing them everywhere. Every. Where.

It was adorable.

One weekend we visited some family and a distant relative remarked, "You'd better break her of that before she goes to kindergarten."

I looked at my sweet little girl—running around the yard, swinging a stick, and pretending to be some sort of scientific superhero—and I immediately dismissed that advice. Break my daughter of her imagination and spirit? I think not.

Even though that conversation took place nearly a year ago, and the goggles have been once again relegated to the dress-up box, I haven't been able to shake it. So today I have a few things to say to my daughter.

Dear Annalyn,

From the moment you were formed you have done the unexpected. From your surprising conception and your refusal to show us your gender during the sonogram to your determination to breathe and eat on your own after just a few days in the NICU (and weeks before you should've entered our world), you've forged your own path and generally done life your way.

And while at times your strong will and unique personality drive me straight up the wall, *I wouldn't change those things about you for the world.*

Just like you tossed aside the chart of developmental milestones for your own timetable, you scoff at society's expectations and silly things like generally accepted fashion standards.

Who cares about the color wheel when you can add one more blinged-out accessory? And who has time to sit still for braids and bows when you can shove a mismatched set of headbands on your head and call it good? And who doesn't need to take a break from princess play to crawl under the dining room table with her tool kit? I mean, really, someone's got to fix it—and Handy Manny isn't showing up anytime soon!

You love pretty, pretty pink and princess everything, but you play doctor and carpenter and scientist just as often. It makes perfect sense for you to perform at a rock concert, complete a science experiment, and create another craft project—all in one day.

And when you work on those craft projects? You chafe against the conventional advice to "stay in the lines," but you can somehow use your safety scissors and glue stick to make a surprisingly realistic rocket ship.

I love these things about you.

Here's the thing, baby girl. I've known since one of my psych classes in college (yes, that long ago) that I'm an extremely high self-monitor, while your dad is way down on the low end of that spectrum. In other words, I notice (and care) a whole lot about what other people are doing, thinking, and feeling, while Dad, well, doesn't.

In those moments when I'm nudging his leg under the table to remind him that we shouldn't say or do *that* in front of *them*, and he responds by asking loudly, "Why did you kick me?" instead of adjusting his behavior or changing the topic, *it puts me over the edge.*

But in those moments when I see you, a miniature version of him in so many ways, stubbornly refuse to wear a hat like every other student on Crazy Hat Day or choose to wear goggles to the farm or a tutu to the grocery store, well, it simply makes me fall in love with both of you even more.

And it makes me want to be like you. Not the girl who cried because her jeans came from Sears and not 5-7-9, and not the girl who wore bangs even though her forehead wasn't made for them and no amount of hair spray could hold their curl or height. It makes me want to be like you, my silly girl who walks to the beat of her own drum, and not the girl who is embarrassed by her small house or plain clothes or twisty career path or plus-size size.

Stay weird, sweet pea. Don't listen to people who say things like, "You should break her of that," or "Why aren't you like everyone else?" You are not everyone else. You were wonderfully and fearfully made by the most creative Creator, and I will take down anyone who wants to squash your uniqueness.

Stay weird, baby girl. Because weird is always better than boring, better than vanilla, better than like-everyone-else.

Stay weird, because not everyone can be weird...just like not everyone can be amazing and world-changing.

Stay weird, no matter what that means.

Stay weird when that means saying "no" when everyone else says "why not?"

Stay weird when that means staying home when everyone else goes to the party, and stay weird when that means trying something new when everyone else is afraid to leave their comfort zone.

Stay weird when you choose an instrument or a sport, and stay weird when you choose a major and a career.

Stay weird when that means putting family first, and stay weird when that means taking time for yourself and that God-sized dream He's given you.

Stay weird when it means joining up, and stay weird when it means standing alone.

Stay weird when it means reading the book instead of seeing the movie.

Stay weird when you save your money or spend it, travel the world or stay close, smile for the picture or make a silly face.

Stay weird when you find the cure, build the house, write the song, or marry the prince.

Stay weird.

Love,
Your mom
(who's just now learning to be happy with her own weirdness)

We are the windows through which our children first see the world. Let us be conscious of the view.

KATRINA KENISON,
Mitten Strings for God: Reflections for Mothers in a Hurry

14

The Little Child Who Leads Me

Leah Highfill

Ohhhh, Mommy!" she gasps. "It's all alone on the floor! It's lonely and cold and it doesn't have a mommy! Oh, the poor little thing. I'm going to put it right up here so it will be safe and warm. There!"

We are standing in my daughter Charity's bedroom as I absent-mindedly give my consent without looking at what she is doing. We don't have much time before we need to leave for skating, and her small and wiggling toddler body needs to be dressed. Pink pants, pink shirt, pink-and-purple-striped hoodie, pink-and-white socks, pink shoes… (pink for dinner, anyone?).

"See, Mommy? I put it there!" She's gasping again, and now her little voice is clamoring for my approval that her good deed not go unnoticed.

Pink outfit in hand, I turn to see what precious creature has captivated my tiny daughter's shower of tender affection. Her hand is gesturing toward the top of her dresser.

It's a leaf.

A leaf, friends. And it isn't even whole. It is a tiny excerpt of a former leaf, mangled and twisted. Definitely dead.

My heart is touched. More than touched—it is smitten, convicted, torn, maybe shattered (in a good way).

A painful thought comes and doesn't want to leave: *My daughter has more compassion for that leaf than I have for most people.*

Compassion flows easily from us and into those we hold most dear. But compassion for the unwhole, the devastated, the piece of life that struggles to grasp hope—this sometimes goes against our very grain as humans. Why are we repelled by that which we are, ourselves, made of? Why do we shrink in fear from the pieces of our own and others' brokenness instead of recognizing the cracks in between those pieces that need the mending agent of tenderness and care?

In Charity's eyes, the leaf was all preciousness. She had not a single thought of where it really belonged or what it really was. I'm awed by my daughter when I see the way she expresses genuine concern for the tiny, the helpless and needy, the broken and struggling, and how she looks for a solution to ease the pain. And of course, she uses logic that makes my heart melt like butter on a sultry day, crippling my ability to refuse her:

That fly that our cat, BoPeep, is stalking for a tasty snack needs to be heroically rescued! "It surely has a family somewhere that needs its help. And how can it help its family if it ends up in BoPeep's tummy?"

That spider who is running for his life should be given a chance to be released into the yard before we flatten him with a shoe! "Don't you know he probably has a mother somewhere who is looking all over for him?!"

That rock she just stepped on is surely feeling more pain from being stepped on than she is experiencing from stepping on said rock. "How would you feel if you were a rock and someone stepped on you?"

She has not a thought of where those things really belong...what they really are. She only feels their pain.

All those things (especially the spider!) are of little worth in the eyes of a not-so-child like me. But in the eyes of a child, they hold great worth. Is it any wonder that Christ issued a special invitation for children to come to Him? I often wonder if He did that in part so that the adult bystanders might be compelled to see what He saw in those children...and to see the wonder in how those children saw Him.

The beauty in the broken and lifeless—it's Christ! It's grace. And it takes the eyes of Christ, the eyes of grace—the eyes of a child—to recognize it.

Oh, this child. This tiny daughter of mine! How she continually humbles me and teaches me and opens my eyes.

How she leads me to become a child again.

Suffer the little children to come unto me, and forbid them not: for of such is the kingdom of God.

MARK 10:14

15

My Daughter Connected My Heart to the World

Tricia Goyer

It never failed that within ten minutes of being at any new setting—a local park, a new class, or a community event—that my daughter Leslie would approach me and introduce me to her new best friend. Leslie was always rail thin as a child, but her personality caused her never to be overlooked. Other children were drawn to her. She was quick to smile and to discover who her new friend was and what she was like. Things didn't change as Leslie got older. Starting the local community college in rural Montana at age 16, Leslie always found herself surrounded by her peers, and as she grew older I was never surprised when Leslie brought a friend home for our family to meet.

I remember the first time Leslie invited a coworker to our home because he had questions about Christianity. Semi was in the United States on a work-study program, and he grew up in a predominately Muslim country.

"He's really nice, Mom. I've been witnessing to him at work. He has a lot of questions, though, and I thought Dad would be able to explain things better." Of course John and I were happy to welcome Semi into our home, and we found out years later that the conversations with my daughter—and us—made a huge impact.

When our family moved to Little Rock, Arkansas, a few years later, Leslie began attending the University of Arkansas in Little Rock. I wasn't surprised when Leslie started bringing home friends right away. I also wasn't surprised that she'd made connections with the International Students, and we met her friends from all over the world: Rwanda, Italy, Brazil, and Sudan, to name a few places. I also wasn't surprised when, after her graduation, Leslie announced she wanted to move overseas as a missionary. It's something she'd been saying she wanted to do since she learned at eight years old that many people hadn't heard about Jesus or the eternal life they could discover through a relationship with Him.

I wish I could say that I fully embraced Leslie's decision, yet the idea that my daughter—who'd just barely became an adult—would live full-time in a foreign country frightened me. Yes, she'd be working with a pastor we knew, but on a daily basis who would be there to help her with culture shock, to assist her with a new language, and most of all, to keep her safe?

Praying for my daughter drew me closer to her—and to God. And the more I prayed, the more I began to understand the intricate ways God works in the world. God used me to impact Leslie, and He used Leslie to open my eyes in new ways.

I was the mom who read missionary stories, but Leslie was the one who moved to foreign soil. I was the one who taught world history and world geography in our homeschool, but Leslie was the one who invited international friends to coffee and listened to their hearts and their struggles. I was the one who felt timid about talking about Jesus with my neighbor, but Leslie was the one who time and time again launched into conversations of faith with other young people from all religions.

And what have I learned from her? No matter where in the world you are from, one's heart's true desire is to simply be known, cared for, and listened to. It doesn't take much to start a conversation with a stranger, just "How are you doing today?" and a desire to truly know the answer.

Leslie's gift of making best friends continues up to this day. My bubbling, little curly-haired girl who used to make a new friend on the slides is now married to a Czech man, teaches English at a foreign university, and opens her home to students from around the world every week through a home Bible study. I often get e-mails like, "Hey, Mom, I just witnessed to three students from Japan who'd never heard about Jesus before. Can you pray for me and for them? We're going to meet again soon to continue our conversation." And so through my daughter I pray for students I'll most likely never get to meet, but whom Leslie meets with week by week, face-to-face.

And even closer to home, Leslie's influence has opened my heart to international women. I remember the first time I met Shamim in a small-group setting. It was clear from her accent that she was from a different country. Instead of thinking of all the ways we were different, I stretched out of my comfort zone to spend time with Shamim, getting to know her better and trying to understand the difficulties of living in our country as an immigrant. I've always been friendly, but I'm learning to open up our home more too. And to really ask questions about people's lives and be attentive to those who see faith differently because of where they were raised.

It makes me think of years ago, a child myself, being in a church service where a missionary asked those who felt called to missions to step forward. Even as I prayed, I hoped deep down that I would *not* be called. As much as I wanted to follow God, I hoped His call would keep me close to home.

And while God has never called me to be an international missionary, Leslie has taught me that all of us are called to love those from the nations wherever we are. Sometimes God calls us to go. Other times He calls us to stay. But either way we are called to love those who are different from us and to open our lives to them. As I've learned from Leslie, a smile and a welcoming attitude can go a long way.

Thou shalt love the Lord thy God with all thy heart, and with all thy soul, and with all thy mind, and with all thy strength: this is the first commandment. And the second is like, namely this, Thou shalt love thy neighbour as thyself. There is none other commandment greater than these.

MARK 12:30-31

16

One of the Most Offensive Things God Asks

Shelly Miller

Water splatters on my shirt as I scrub the last bits of garlic, tomatillos, and cilantro from the Cuisinart with intensity. The crunching sound of a key pushing into the lock interrupts my focus and shifts my gaze from the kitchen sink to the front door. I quickly turn off the faucet, and before I can dry soapy hands on a dish towel, she walks into the house. Glowing.

My daughter, Murielle, is home for a long weekend from an art and design college a few states away. I haven't heard that sound of a key turning in the lock for a month. In a matter of moments, our arms intertwine, embracing.

"Are you happy to be home?" I whisper in her ear.

"Yes, I'm so excited," she replies.

She didn't pack a suitcase because every garment she owns is scrunched in the vast recesses of a laundry bag. And I've never been so happy to wash and fold dirty clothes in my life.

As she walks into her bedroom carrying a backpack of art supplies for homework, she exclaims, "Whoa, it's so empty in here. This feels weird."

Almost as weird as her absence on the couch, at the dinner table, and in the driveway.

I swipe a soppy dishrag into stray pieces of lettuce on the countertop while she and her dad unload the last things from the car. Walking past the bar with a blanket draped over her shoulder, she looks at me and says, "This doesn't need to be washed. I brought it with me because I want it to smell like home when I go back to my dorm room."

It's hard to believe it's been three years since experiencing my daughter's first weekend from college back into familiar family rhythms.

The sparse appearance of her bedroom was a shock at first glance because while she was beginning a new season as a college student, the rest of us were preparing for life abroad in England. Souvenirs from adventures and a menagerie of artwork were decorating her dorm room while decades of childhood memories left behind were slowly being boxed up and stacked in a storage unit.

If I thought the absence of my firstborn was odd three years ago, time has sobered me into a concoction of vague grief and consolation. Now it's not only stretches of pavement that will separate us, but an entire ocean.

Letting go of our children is perhaps one of the most offensive things God asks of parents. It's the same kind of surrender required when God decides rescue isn't what is best for us. When we feel desperate and out of sorts, waiting is God's big ask. *Will you wait for Me to work all things together for your good?*

On Mother's Day, we talked to Murielle, her rosy cheeks and bright green eyes front and center on the flat screen. Her dad and I were seated in the wingback chairs in the living room in another country while she snuggled under that same blanket, the smell of home starkly different yet still comforting.

Holding up pieces of artwork to the camera, she revealed the latest masterpiece created in short snatches of time between long work hours and sorting laundry. She was glowing as God's face shined upon her.

She asked advice about purchasing brake pads for her car and debated different ways of approaching her boss with hard questions. While I listened to her dad's wisdom in response, I vacillated between grief over not being present to help her practically and the consolation of maturity I was witnessing due to the physical distance between us.

Rebirth took place when I discovered that the life I envisioned for my firstborn is realized, not because I have controlled outcomes or provided safety and security, but because, in my absence, God's presence is sure.

Didn't he set us on the road to life?
Didn't he keep us out of the ditch?
He trained us first,
passed us like silver through refining fires,
Brought us into hardscrabble country,
pushed us to our very limit,
Road-tested us inside and out,
took us to hell and back;
Finally he brought us
to this well-watered place.

PSALM 66:10-12 MSG

My mother's heart longs to provide rescue, but to interrupt the refining process is to delay the fulfillment of God's purpose within her. The place of abundance requires choosing risks over safety. And the psalmist reminds me that silver is tried seven times.

A refiner knows the intensity of a flame required to try silver. He watches with keen assessment as impurities rise to the surface for skimming. Only the refiner of our soul discerns with accuracy when the process is finished, when He sees His face reflected in the heart of His work.

Become helpless in controlling the destiny of your children and discover how God is parenting them in becoming the people He envisioned when they took their first breath. He works all things together for our good (Romans 8:28).

The face of Jesus is a face that belongs to us the way our past belongs to us. It is a face that we belong to if only as to the one face out of the past that has perhaps had more to do with the shaping of our present than any other.

FREDERICK BUECHNER

17

What Am I Telling Her? A Mother's Message to Her Daughters

Alexandra Kuykendall

"Mom, you don't have to be perfect!" I sensed a tension in her tone, but I was unsure the reason. Judgment? Disappointment? Recognition of hypocrisy personified right in front of her?

My gaze moved from the mirror and landed on this girl standing next to me. This mini-me. This one watching and figuring out what it means to be a woman. And then my gaze moved to my bed and the pile of shirts I'd tried on but discarded as unworthy for the outfit I'd wear to church that morning. And then again on this girl whose face asked, *Are you really so concerned about how you look that you're willing to make us late?*

This business of raising girls, of giving and re-giving messages of their value, falls on us mothers. We try with all we can muster to counter the memos the world passes out that say you must…

You must have a distinct waistline and legs that stretch out like skyscrapers.

You must have clear skin and smooth hair.

You must have the latest trends wrapped around your shoulders and hanging from your bony hips.

You must have a smile stretched across those lips, no matter the feelings inside.

We do everything but hold their shoulders and scream at them so we are louder than these messages. So we are heard. So we out-message the marketers and out-shout the mean girls at school. To tell them they are created in the Creator's image. He made them to reflect His beauty. His love. His goodness.

Daily I tell my daughters, "You are beautiful." "Your differences are okay." "You matter."

But my words are only as effective as my actions.

I look in the mirror with all kinds of criticism ready to spill out. Why does my stomach pooch out that way? Why does my face have so many blotches on it? Why do these pants pull right here? Why did I say that? Why didn't I say something else? I fixate on my imperfections with four pairs of eyes watching my every move and listening to every word. I may scream how beautiful they are, but what if I haven't absorbed it for myself? Will they really believe it if their number one model of womanhood says one thing about them but believes another about herself?

I already believe they are beautiful, but part of my raising them is modeling a woman whose life speaks the same language as her words. Here is my challenge today to us moms of beauties: take back that mirror time and read the passage from Scripture below out loud. Because if we want our girls to believe this about themselves, we must pull these words out and believe them for ourselves.

It may sound cheesy or forced. That's okay; that means we are doing something new.

Moms, may our hearts absorb these words. Now speak them aloud and believe them for you.

Oh yes, you shaped me first inside, then out;
you formed me in my mother's womb.
I thank you, High God—you're breathtaking!
Body and soul, I am marvelously made!
I worship in adoration—what a creation!

You know me inside and out,
you know every bone in my body;
You know exactly how I was made, bit by bit,
how I was sculpted from nothing into something.

Like an open book,
you watched me grow from conception to birth;
all the stages of my life were spread out before you,
The days of my life all prepared
before I'd even lived one day.

PSALM 139:13-16 MSG

18

I Am My Mother's Daughter

Alia Joy

I help to situate her after she's wheeled back from X-ray. Her face hushed in pain, teeth gritted, face hollowed out and wincing. She lets out a slow and shaky exhale and I blink back my tears, but one escapes and rolls from my chin, plopping obscenely on her hospital gown and staining her with my grief.

I came from her body. And maybe this is why her pain resonates in me. When she lies shattered in the hospital bed, it's why I keep checking behind the curtain to see if someone will come ease her suffering. If someone will bear witness to the brokenness in her back. Nurses sit typing at stations. People wander by, checking charts and wheeling patients. Every cubicle is occupied, every room filled with people gathered in pain.

I hate hospitals.

I was five when they told her I might die. When they told her to hope for the best, but prepare for the worst. I was a tiny birdlike girl with a spine so bruised it blossomed like a dahlia in yellows and violets and then the dull brown of dying blood.

My blood was no good. The blood of my marrow. My sick spine.

Tiny wig stands had lined the ward's bedside tables, Styrofoam statues standing guard over so many tiny bareheaded children grasping at the edges of life.

As a dying girl, I would reach for my mama, and she would be at my side even as I rolled toward her. She watched, helpless, when I cried as they poked and prodded, and she never sobbed over me, but how she must have longed to. Instead, she smoothed my hair back from my tears as her fingers swam through my strands. The feel of my mother's competent hands in my hair, like a fish in the waves, soothed me back to the place I came from. I was a girl full of life; I was her girl.

I don't know when she found the time for her tears. I only know she soaked up every one of mine.

But now I cannot hold mine back, and they spring up clumsily as the hours tick by. I swipe at them and she soothes me. She is still mothering me, even now. Some roles are hard to reverse.

We wait for the doctor to come back and tell us what we already suspect. She has broken her back. A compost cart toppled on her while she was gardening and she was crushed beneath it. We wait. Six hours pass with her body crumpled on the hospital gurney before the doctor tells her she fractured her T11 and T12 vertebrae. Only then does he offer a shot to ease the constant torment. He plans to brace her and get her on her way. He dismisses us without ever really seeing her at all. When she rises, her hair is matted. She looks like a girl. I turn away so she doesn't see my tears fall.

There is no room for her brokenness here. The ER is full.

I am her nurse.

At home I gather her things from her room and arrange them on my husband, Josh's, nightstand. He sleeps on the couch while I feed her and help her to the bathroom and wake with her at night to offer cool sips of water. I break open the child safety cap and shake out pills flat on my palm like I'm feeding a sparrow. She takes them into her body, and I pray they'll heal her. I hear the moan of unbearable agony as she waits for it to dull the pain. Inside I doubt the God who would drag us back to the brink when I was barely hanging on to begin with. I am thankful there is no spinal damage and she will heal in time. But I am angry I have to be thankful for what feels like scraps from the master's table. God's goodness and sufficiency seem wholly inadequate when my mom is reduced to brokenness's ragged edge.

I want wholeness for us and I want it now. I have forgotten what it is to be healed.

I shield her from my burdens because I'm supposed to be the one caring for her. When I start to feel my mind unraveling, I load dishes absently into the dishwasher, I keep stuffing laundry in the dryer, and I watch while my whole mad world spins wildly on. I try to stay present in my body, present in my mind.

I want to care for her like she's always cared for me. When I was a little girl and the nurses came in the darkness and the room flooded with the harsh fluorescent light and my plastic bracelet held me captive to needle pricks and cold, hard fingers and nurses who forgot how to smile for small broken children, she stroked my hair and whispered lullabies into my pillow.

I turn on the showerhead and check the temperature like a new mother dipping her elbow into her baby's bathwater. Then I undress her carefully. My hands reach out to hold her arms like two partners about to dance, and I hold her steady as she gets into the shower. I work the water through her hair and down her back, where her spine is swollen and bruised. Our bodies are familiar, and I remember we've done this before.

Muscle memory recalls the days when hands healed and comforted and drew tears away from broken places. Our spines have taught us to hold each other up when our worlds go crooked and spoil.

My hands work the shampoo into her roots, the raven strands graying at her temples, and I'm careful to be gentle as she tips her head back like she might see God. This is all I can offer. I am my mother's daughter. I am still her girl, and she taught me to love through the darkest nights, when all we can do is surrender to the pain in the world and find some solace that even then we can offer our whole selves as a salve. Our hands are miracles to a hurting world.

Healing comes in so many forms.

As I rinse the suds from her hair, I remember what it is to live healed. I remember.

We hold each other up in the face of brokenness. I remember, because I am my mother's daughter.

Courage is not having the strength to go on; it is going on when you don't have the strength.

THEODORE ROOSEVELT

Part 4

A Mother's Hope

Youth fades, love droops, the leaves of friendship fall; a mother's secret hope outlives them all.

OLIVER WENDELL HOLMES SR.,
A Mother's Secret

19

Sign on the Dotted Line

KariAnne Wood

No one warns you.

Having twins is a lot like a ride on an upside-down roller coaster. One minute you're slowly but surely ticking away to the top of the ride. And then? Five seconds later the cart almost takes off without you and you're suddenly flipped around with your arms flailing in the wind, hands holding on for dear life.

One evening, about two weeks after the twins were born, I stood in the middle of my living room, bleary-eyed from lack of sleep with seven-day hair, wearing pajamas covered in spit-up as I wailed plaintively to my mother.

"How can I do this?"

"I'm not going to make it."

"They are totally winning."

Exhausted, I wiped my face, brushed the hair away from my eyes, inhaled and exhaled several times, and then stood patiently waiting for her words of wisdom. I knew she'd have an answer. My mother has successfully raised five children. She is brilliant and experienced and wise and has never met a good piece of advice she didn't like.

But for once, she didn't say a word.

She just took one look at me and laughed. Then she paused, wiped her eyes, and laughed some more. Finally, she offered up this sage piece of wisdom that made my heart beat faster and my palms sweat and shivers run up and down my spine.

"This is nothing. Just wait till they're teenagers."

That was 12 years ago, and I've never forgotten her words. Sometimes I'd look at those cherubic faces and sweet smiles and tiny hands tucked into mine and bright blue eyes so full of wonder and joy, and I'd hear her words again. I'd listen to those little voices, chirping out the funniest things that made me smile, and I'd think about what she'd said.

Was it possible?

Could they?

Would they one day roll their eyes and say things like, "Whatever" and "Really, Mom" and "I am so sure"? Would they toss their hair and stomp their feet and demand a tattoo and jeans full of holes that cost $200? Would those tiny hands one day wear orange nail polish and rainbow glitter?

But why borrow trouble? Why even bring it up? Why give anyone ideas about what might be ahead on the horizon? I wasn't even sure that those tiny girls understood that sometimes being a teenager might be challenging for parents. So I kept my questions and worries and concerns all to myself.

Or so I thought.

The other day the twins tromped into the kitchen, whispering and laughing—hiding something (unsuccessfully) behind their backs.

"Umm…Mom? We have something we wrote. Something we want to show you that will make you feel better so you won't ever have to worry." Two sets of sparkling blue eyes looked at each other conspiratorially and then smiled at me with mischievous grins. "This is for you, Mom." One of my daughters giggled as she handed me a piece of paper.

It was a one-day-I'm-going-to-be-a-really-nice-teenager contract.

The contract was written on a purple piece of paper covered with hearts and polka dots. Scrawled across the front of it in perfect cursive handwriting were the following words:

I promise you that I will try to be a good and nice teenager.

And if I am not...you may pull out this contract and show me.

I will try to be nice and kind to all people around me and follow rules and the Ten Commandments.

Thank you for your appreciation.

At the end of the contract next to a heart with a smiley face, both of the twins had signed and dated it. Everything looked official.

I wanted to laugh.

I wanted to cry.

I wanted to call my mother and tell her she was wrong. Those upcoming teenage years? They were shaping up to be a breeze. What could go wrong now? I had a contract.

But I didn't pick up the phone. Instead, I sent a silent prayer toward heaven. I thanked God for sending me a little humor for the road ahead. I knew it wouldn't always be easy. I understood now that having teenagers comes with its own set of challenges. There would be sleepless nights and buckets of worry and new obstacles to overcome—and seven-day hair that might or might not make a repeat appearance.

It all happens so fast. One minute you're filling sippy cups and replacing binkies and preparing a three-course meal of Cheerios and apple juice. Then you blink and someone is asking you for mascara.

The roller coaster is still turning me upside down. I'm twisting and looping and spinning and just trying to keep my eyes on the road ahead. I think our family is going to make it. But just in case—just on the off chance we get offtrack along the way—I've still got my seat belt buckled.

And I'm keeping that contract in a very safe place.

There are two things in life for which we
are never truly prepared: twins.

JOSH BILLINGS

20

Grace Notes

Dawn Camp

Her middle name is Graycen, and she's the only one of our children who doesn't have a family name borrowed from an ancestor before her. We wanted something reminiscent of grace, but rather than the more masculine Grayson, we added an unnecessary-but-winsome *y* in the center. Artistic license is more permissible in a middle name, after all. An older brother who possesses a similarly placed *y* informed us that it never did him any good, but we were not dissuaded. Her first name makes a brief appearance in 1 Corinthians 1:11, so it's slightly biblical too.

I nicknamed Chloe "the drama queen" at an early age because of her animated nature. Our little Southern belle, she dropped the *r* sound after vowels when she spoke. With her big eyes and soft curls, she resembled a Madame Alexander doll come to life.

Although the years have passed, her flair for the dramatic hasn't. It's a roll of the dice which Chloe we might see from day to day. If hormones during pregnancy made me nauseated, crave everything from tomatoes to Slurpees to orange juice to naps, and experience an assortment of other related quirks, it's no wonder they produce dramatic results in a teen.

Sometimes Chloe and I butt heads; much of what I say or do irritates her. An unseen cloud hovers in the air between us, distorting the words from my mouth as they enter her ears. But in her defense, I misread her meaning just as often. I don't remember empathy for my parents being one of my more dominant traits as a teen, so she probably doesn't worry a lot about my perspective.

Thankfully, when she does, sometimes she writes a letter.

As a preteen she penned what I call the Sorry Letter. It began, "Dear Mom, i'm so sorry for allways being so rude and mean," and ended with "all I'm saying is i'm sorry, and i hope you will forgive me!" followed by two checkboxes, one for yes and one for no. The two-page letter contained the word *sorry* 12 times. Twelve. Sorry for being a bad sister, lazy in school, whining, being disrespectful; she even said she was sorry for not always eating the food I put in front of her.

On days when motherhood is rough, when I want to toss in the proverbial towel, letters like this make a difference. A child who shows evidence of a contrite heart and a repentant spirit gives a parent hope.

In this year's Father's Day letter, Chloe told my husband: "One day you'll get a call from a hospital notifying you that your beautiful daughter has died in an awful skateboard accident or a shark attack or something, and you'll instantly regret ever saying no to me when I ask you for things." (Along with a flair for the dramatic, she shares the sense of adventure and fearlessness I held at her age.) Her letter then moved from the silly to the serious, in some of the sweetest words ever written from a daughter to her father. My husband should frame it.

This year's Mother's Day letter began with the lighthearted side of Chloe at her best: "Happy Mother's Day to someone who carried me for 9 months physically and who will for like 30 years financially." Most of her notes to me start with a silly declaration that she is both a brat and my favorite child, but usually conclude with a sweet sentiment that pulls my heartstrings. If I might assume she's too wrapped up in her own life to notice mine, she proves otherwise with notes like this:

> Mom,
>
> All the kids have been saying that you seem stressed out, so here's some stress away, candy, lotion, and a candle to help you relax! We love you and you don't get enough credit.

How often does a teenage daughter tell her mother she doesn't get enough credit? (The answer: almost never.)

I'm thankful for these scribbled impressions, like a mirror to her soul: a sweet glimpse of what lies beneath the surface and a view of what's ahead, beyond teenage hormones and mother-daughter clashes.

And it's so worth the wait.

They that wait upon the L*ORD* *shall renew their strength; they shall mount up with wings as eagles; they shall run, and not be weary; and they shall walk, and not faint.*

ISAIAH 40:31

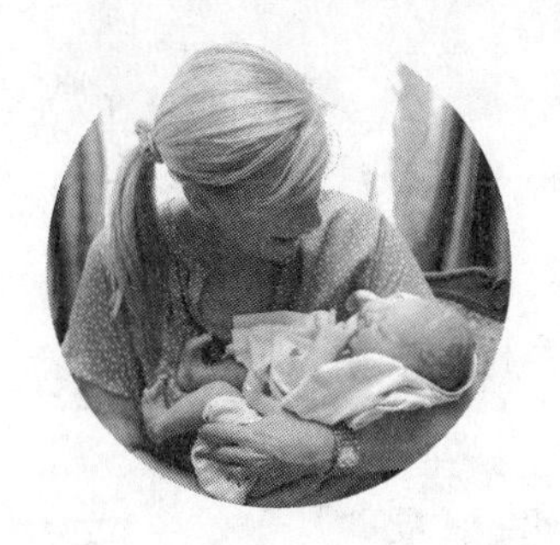

21
A New Granddaughter, and a Few Thoughts

Rachel Anne Ridge

I had the privilege of being with my daughter, Lauren, her husband, Robert, and my granddaughter Ivy (age two) for the first five days of my new granddaughter, Hazel's, life.

I have almost no words for the wonder of this new life, brought into the world by my daughter, but I'll try today.

You see, there's this *feeling*.

I've experienced it three times now, with each new grandbaby, as I looked at my daughters with their pink bundles in their arms. Perhaps it's because my girls have had daughters that I've felt this way—I don't know.

Maybe it's a rite of passage.

But I look at Lauren. It's like I'm seeing her through glasses with magic lenses: I see her as the beautiful, grown-up woman that she is, while simultaneously seeing her younger self—the child who loved to draw pictures and whose hands were always creating something out of found objects. Bits of string, shoe boxes, paper, and tape...always lots of tape.

Somehow I feel her little arms around my neck and remember the stories we read at bedtime and the kites we flew in the field behind our house. Cookies and milk after school, the piles of dishes and laundry that I could never really get control of.

The years of work and love, and confidence and doubt.

I see it all, images overlaying images; some faded around the edges, but still vivid and full of color.

I see myself too. I see how I obsessed about whether I was doing a good enough job as a mom. Was I serving enough vegetables? Was I teaching the right life lessons? Did I lose my patience too many times? Did I make the right educational choices? Did I let her wear mismatched socks way too often?

My magic glasses fade away, and here is Lauren, holding out her new baby for the two-year-old to kiss.

And I know all the years of work, and love, and confidence, and doubt are ahead of her as well.

I kiss the top of *my* baby's head. My beautiful girl, this young mama.

And I press her close. I want to say this, but I can't speak:

All of the wonder is ahead of you too, honey.

Hold on tight for the ride.

It's wonderful and messy and hard and good. You'll question yourself a million times along the way. You'll stay up late praying. You'll be overcome with joy a million more times.

It will feel like a spinning Tilt-A-Whirl sometimes.

But listen, don't worry.

Motherhood is supposed to be this way.

And one day, a couple of decades from now, you'll find a pair of magic glasses in your pocket that lets you see the past and the present all at the same time.

You'll see how Hazel and Ivy grew into beautiful mamas, and how they invited you to spend the first few days with them and their new babies because they needed you to help them settle in. You'll marvel at their patience, their ability to watch *Daniel Tiger's Neighborhood* with toddlers for hours, their kindness and generosity and love.

And you'll still feel their little arms around your neck, and be able to see the kites and the cookies, and hear the sleepy whispers at bedtime.

You'll remember your doubts. You'll remember how you sometimes worried, and you'll see now that you shouldn't have.

Because now you see how it all turned out, and the sheer beauty of it catches you, holds you, and leaves you breathless in its wake.

You'll feel so very proud of those kids you didn't ruin with the mismatched sock thing.

You'll see just how amazing they are.

And you'll feel simply...grateful.

Being a mother is learning about strengths
you didn't know you had, and dealing
with fears you didn't know existed.

LINDA WOOTEN

22

The Miracle of a Daughter: A Birth of Hope

Leah Highfill

"You've got a million-dollar family right there!" If we've heard it once, we've heard it a thousand times from random strangers in a store, on the street, in the park.

My husband and I smile our thanks, then wink at each other, our looks conveying volumes.

If you had spoken into my girlish dreams of motherhood and told me that the process of having children would be devastating and fraught with medical trauma, I probably wouldn't have believed you. But the path God chose for my husband and me became an intense trial of our faith, a crucible that broke us and squeezed everything out of us.

We had been married five months when I found out I was expecting our first child. We enjoyed about five days of elation before I landed in the hospital, fighting for my life and my baby's life. After twenty weeks of trial and error—both in and out of the hospital—I was diagnosed with severe hyperemesis gravidarum, a rare pregnancy condition that causes intense, unrelenting physical suffering and has no cure. We were told multiple times to either get an abortion or prepare for the death of myself and/or our developing baby. In the attempt to control the symptoms, my doctors put me on maxed-out doses of several medications that cancer patients use. By the time my husband and I reached our one-year wedding anniversary, we were drowning in massive medical debt from multiple hospital stays, ambulance rides, specialists, and costly medications.

Every day was a wild roller coaster of fear and hope. Our life looked nothing like the girlish dreams of motherhood that I had entertained. We were struggling to breathe in every way—physically, mentally, emotionally, spiritually, financially.

When our baby boy was born healthy, our team of doctors gave praise to God, acknowledging a medical miracle. My health was shattered, and our doctors warned us to "never try that again."

Recovery from my traumatic pregnancy and birth was long and bumpy, but hope is hard to kill. I studied my diagnosis as if I had an impending exam. I wanted to understand the condition. But more than that, I was searching for hope—for success stories that would point the way for us to definitely "try that again."

Once everything was in place for an active care plan, I joined a medical study on hyperemesis gravidarum that Canada was conducting at the time. And we "tried that again."

Once more we had about five days of elation over the two pink lines before I found myself staring at the ceiling of a hospital room. As if on repeat, we faced the medical trauma, the debt, the ongoing uncertainty for our survival.

I was crushed. I had searched and prayed and believed that it would be better the second time around—that we could actually enjoy the process of having a family instead of focusing so much on just staying alive.

One day in the middle of a life that consisted of hospitalizations, bedrest, medication regimens, physical suffering, and deep struggle and disappointment, I heard a sentence during a routine appointment that changed my life forever:

"You're having a little girl."

Months later, two weeks early, our little Charity came into the world quickly—after just forty-five minutes of labor and our doctor rushing in from the hockey rink to catch her—and I'm still amazed at how healing her actual birthing process was for me. She was a delightful baby and continues to bring so much joy to our family.

Our daughter is nine years old at the time of this writing. And yet this experience of fighting for and birthing a daughter remains one of the most profound of my life. It was the birth of a miracle daughter, yes. But it was the birth of so many other valuable gifts. It was God birthing hope in me where hope had died. It was God building faith in me where faith greatly shook. It was God washing a significant healing through me where pain and suffering had wreaked havoc on our life in every possible way. It was God making a dream come true where dreams had long laid down their banners.

Sometimes million-dollar families come easily. And other times they defy all odds and break through the devastation, giving birth to hope. Hope is born through hopelessness. Joy comes on wings through suffering. Healing washes over pain. The best gifts are given from sacrifice. Life emerges from death. Beauty rises from ashes.

The God of hope makes sure of it.

Faith is the substance of things hoped for, the evidence of things not seen.

HEBREWS 11:1

23

A Motherhood Story of Hope

Holley Gerth

I'd like to tell you a story.

It starts with a wedding, a boy and a girl standing at the altar. They said, "I do" and it seemed so simple. Years later when they thought about having children, they said, "We will" and thought it would be the same. Only it wasn't. Instead of picking out pink or blue onesies, they stared month after month at single pink lines on pregnancy tests.

There were tears and prayers, moments of anger and frustration, loss of a little one who slipped to heaven before even a "hello" on earth. They wondered what having a family would look like for them, if maybe they had done something wrong or been disqualified.

Then one night the girl watched a special on television about foster kids who age out of the system, who are told at 18, "Have a nice life." And she wondered who would cheer for them at their college graduation, walk them down the aisle, or rock their babies, who they would call when they lost a job or just had a bad day. "That's not okay," she said. "Not okay at all."

In the meantime, God showed her that she didn't have to be a physical mother to still be a mama. In Genesis 3:20, Eve is called "the mother of all living." All women are mothers, she discovered, because all women bring life into the world in some way. So she birthed books and her friends threw her a book shower. She got to mother women all over the world with her words. She started to heal, but there was still a place deep inside saved for someone. She prayed for her child who was out there somewhere without knowing a name or face.

Years went by and she was invited to a banquet at Saving Grace, a place for girls who age out of the foster system or would otherwise be homeless. She met a 20-year-old young woman that night, and she knew almost right away, *This is my daughter*. Her husband agreed.

It took time. There were lunches and conversations and hugs and misunderstandings and prayers, and they did the awkward dance of becoming family until they knew it by heart. One day that girl, Lovelle, moved into their guest bedroom, took their last name, called them "Mom and Dad."

Later Lovelle met a boy, and her dad walked her down the aisle in a white dress. She and the groom said, "I do" too.

More time passed. Last fall Lovelle called, emotion in her voice. "Mom, I'm pregnant," she said. And I almost dropped the phone because this story is mine. I'm going to be a grandma. Just last week I sat next to my daughter at another banquet for Saving Grace. I leaned over and placed my hand on her beautiful belly. And I felt a flutter, my granddaughter saying "hello" for the first time.

My eyes filled with tears. I thought of Mark and me on our wedding day, all those pink lines, meeting Lovelle, becoming a family, her wedding day too, and the moment I found out we would be grandparents. Then I imagined what years from now may hold as I watch that little girl grow up—story times and bubble baths and trips to the zoo to see long-necked giraffes. Oh, there is so much yet to be.

If your motherhood journey doesn't look the way you wanted it to, I want you to know I've been there. I wish I could wrap an arm around your shoulder, take you out for coffee, listen long and hard. This is what I know for sure: there is hope, and this chapter is not over yet. It may not look like what you imagined, but it will be good because the One writing it is.

And if your motherhood journey is in a season of celebration right now, then I am joining in with you. As a daughter, a mama, a grandma, a woman who has come to understand what extravagant grace looks like. I will wrap my arms around my family today, and I will place my hand on my daughter's beautiful belly again. I will be grateful, so grateful, that nothing turned out the way I planned.

Proper stories seem to close with "The End," but this one feels like it's still only the beginning. There is so much more to come. *I can't wait to meet you, little one.*

Yes, we are *all* mothers in some way today. And we are all part of the great story of motherhood God is writing from generation to generation, from Eve to eternity.

However motherhood comes to you, it's a miracle.

VALERIE HARPER

24

What's in a Name?

Dawn Camp

I will always connect the birth and early days of my third daughter, Felicity, with the last days of my mother. Although I gave birth in the middle of the night, Mother was there to meet her new granddaughter. Everyone in the delivery room could tell she wouldn't live to see this child run and play, to grow and bloom, and so time and routine were suspended as I passed my newborn daughter to her grandmother before she was bathed or measured, weighed or fed. My mother held her while I hemorrhaged, unseen.

I didn't nurse Felicity right away or have the external, postdelivery uterine massage that I always hated. Either of them, or ideally both, would have caused contractions and stopped the bleeding. It was after Mother left when I realized I couldn't stand up or walk on my own and we knew there was a problem. I broke out in a cold sweat, like during the transitional phase of labor I'd gone through such a short time ago, while my blood pressure dropped rapidly.

The nurses blew one vein after another, desperately trying to insert an IV, as my husband and I looked at each other and wondered what was happening to me. A third nurse entered the room, and I insist to this day—although I admit the possibility of delusion—that her last name was Hand. I read the word on her nametag and looked into her warm, brown eyes, and something inside me whispered that hers were the hands that could save me. She inserted the needle on the first try and fluids flooded my body, along with the medicine that caused the contractions necessary to stop further bleeding.

The next morning my midwife, who had gone home before the excitement began, asked whether I'd thought it would be better to bleed to death than have that awful tummy massage. "Maybe" was my reply. She said my uterus was old and tired (which wasn't a very nice thing to say) and therefore hadn't clamped down on its own and stopped the bleeding. It was, after all, my seventh delivery; I still consider it my best (except for the hemorrhaging part, of course). Mother was sick and surely didn't need to know what occurred after she left the hospital. "This never happened," I told my husband. It was better that way.

Mother was initially skeptical about our choice of names, although we gave our daughter her middle one, Anne, and added the extra *e* she had always wanted. She thought Felicity sounded like electricity and people would associate it with the TV show of the same name, which ran for four seasons and ended the year before our daughter was born. We never saw the show and weren't worried about it, or the American Girl doll either. I posted a birth announcement online, which included the definition of *felicity* from Webster's 1828 dictionary: "happiness, or rather great happiness; blessedness; blissfulness; appropriately, the joys of heaven." My mother called to say she couldn't imagine giving a child a name with a better meaning and never questioned it again.

Five months later Mother's health deteriorated and she spent three weeks living at home with weekly visits from hospice care. My sister, her seven-year-old daughter, and Felicity and I moved in with my parents. Our oldest son was 18 and a senior in high school, so he took care of our other children at home. My husband checked on them after work and then spent nights with us; I needed the support. Members of our church brought food to my parents' house, and members of our homeschool group brought it to my kids. Our people carried us through this hard time.

Every day was different. Some days Mother didn't wake up (and we wondered if she ever would), and some days she smiled and talked. One day Felicity lay in her pack 'n play in the room where we slept and laughed and cooed as she discovered her voice. The sound echoed throughout the upstairs and down the hall to my parents' room, where it reached my mother's ears. There are few things as contagious as a baby's laughter, and Felicity's brought the kind of joy that was foretold by her name. Although her grandmother passed away when she was six months old, Felicity's presence lightened her final days.

Now our girl is almost 14, and the word most used to describe her is *sweet.* We hear it from teachers, neighbors, other parents, church friends. She's the tallest female in our family, a fact that she will not allow us to forget. She's started wearing makeup, but she still sleeps with Snicklefritz, a ragged but much-loved pink bear she received as a gift at her birth. I wish for Felicity the blessedness and blissfulness we hoped to bestow in her name; that she will continue to bring happiness to those around her and that she will cling to joy—and the One who is its source—always.

What's in a name? That which we call a rose
by any other name would smell as sweet.

WILLIAM SHAKESPEARE,
Romeo and Juliet

Part 5

The Strength of the Single Mother

Strength and honour are her clothing; and she shall rejoice in time to come.

PROVERBS 31:25

25

Mama Faced the Sink

Wendy Speake

I can see the gentle side-to-side sway of my mama's hips as she stirred the batter. Leaning over the bowl, she worked out lumps until they disappeared. Into the oven went cookies, cake, or some other deliciousness. Then Mama faced the sink.

Steam rose and bubbles formed as she pulled on her old yellow gloves. Hands plunged and scrubbed and made things clean again. The counter was last to be washed down, until the white tile sparkled.

With that she turned to me and smiled, went to the oven, and checked on that night's dessert. Mama always served dessert. A single mom has to have priorities about what to keep and what to let go. But she never let dessert slide, even when it was just us three.

My brother sat across the kitchen table from me, and Mama sat to my side. Sweet and sour pork chops and barbecued ribs were my favorites; then came dessert. Lemon bars and chocolate chip cookies, brownies and cheesecake, those were some of her best.

When we had guests, I helped set the dining room table. An ironed tablecloth and crisp linen napkins, accentuated by candles and low-lying plants. When she really wanted things special, Mama would have me polish the leaves on the centerpiece with a soft cloth and a spray bottle of Windex, then I'd melt down the old wax from the glass votives before adding new candles. I learned young how to order utensils in their rightful place, when to fill water glasses, and where each guest should be seated.

The placement of our dinner guests was paramount; subtly orchestrated, but never mentioned. Guests always faced the living room. The fireplace, cascading houseplants, and inviting fireside seats that would cradle after-dinner conversations bid them welcome. But my mama... Mama and I sat side by side, and we faced the kitchen.

Though her kitchen was always clean and pots and pans were put away before dinner guests arrived, she never wanted them facing the fluorescent reality of her sink. She gave them her best.

Thirty years later she still leads me by example. But today, when we visit her quaint home, downsized though lovely as ever, I am her most honored guest. Her daughter. Because I am privy to Mama's secrets, I accept the seat she offers me at her table, with my back to the kitchen, as the love offering it is.

Then Mama...Mama faces the sink.

Today I work to pass that legacy of hospitable love down to my own children, whipping up Mama's recipes and inviting my kids to set the table when guests are coming. When we host a large dinner party, I cram them in on the far side of the table. Most assuredly not the place of honor, as they give the most comfortable seats to friends and neighbors.

I also strive as an author and speaker to host my online and conference "friends" with the same generous preference. Denying the seat of honor, so to speak, and sitting instead with guests who've purchased tickets, pouring their tea. However, one afternoon at a local church's springtime luncheon it wasn't my simple example that shone brightest.

It's my habit to arrive early to these events, as hostesses set their tables. Linens and bouquets are offered up as fragrant offerings to their guests. Once I'm hooked up to a microphone and told when I'll be introduced, I walk the room. Ladies bedeck each place setting with family china and crystal, adding thoughtful party favors and placards beside each teacup. Some are extravagant, others simple; a tall glass vase of hydrangeas, or a small spray of roses from one's garden.

On that particular afternoon, as I enjoyed these preparty rituals before guests arrived, I overheard two women talking. They were co-hosting a large, round table for their mutual friends. One of the two said, "Here, let's take these two seats now, so we have the best view." The other meekly responded, "Why don't we take these ones instead?" Walking to the opposite side of the table, she pulled out the chairs that had their backs completely to the stage.

My mother would have nodded.

Preference is part of our family motto to this day. Our children have learned it in our family mission statement: "We honor our parents, preferring and encouraging others, always serving the least of these." Living it out isn't easy. I understand what a struggle it can be to lay down your life each day as a mother and wife, and choose instead to give your best to others. But let me encourage you today with my words, as my mother encouraged me by her example, to do just that.

Face the sink.

Oh, the joy that service and sacrifice afford both the giver and the gifted.

And there is power, sweet friend, in your most simple, sacrificial offerings. Generational power. Not only are you offering the best you have to give to your children, you're setting an example for your daughters each time you face the sink and put others before yourself.

Face the sink where you are. I'll be practicing the same love over here where God has me.

Use hospitality one to another without grudging.

1 PETER 4:9

26

Unintentional Lessons

Robin Dance

I remember Mama's king-size bed, an indoor playground for a child.

Its headboard, a garish marriage of gold leaf and carved pressboard, was a perfect balance beam for size-one feet. My sister and I would mount it from the gray, four-drawer metal filing cabinet off to one side, scale its length with the wall as our never-miss "spotter," then dismount by tiptoeing onto the bedside table or, in adventuresome moments, cannonballing onto the middle of the mattress.

The bed was a slippery splash of polyester and pink roses, the embodiment of beauty and sophistication and style to my little girl eyes. (Adult eyes recall '60s synthetic delusion.)

Atop her rose garden refuge one day, lying on her side and playing with my baby brother, my mother's world stopped spinning: she discovered a lump in her breast. Some might have dismissed it or not noticed it at all. Mama didn't have that luxury—breast cancer had taken the life of her mother when she herself was just a baby.

Her diagnosis was confirmed, and her prognosis? A death warrant. Given less than a year to live, she was now on borrowed time.

> Courage is almost a contradiction in terms. It means a strong desire to live taking the form of readiness to die (G.K. Chesterton).

Mama grew up in rural Georgia, and circumstances early in life calloused her with determination and strength. She was stubborn and feisty and deliberate. A sweet friend of mine once said, "I had cancer, but it didn't have me." That's how Mama faced it too. Obstinately shaking her clenched fist in the face of the demon, she vowed to live five more years so my brother—her baby—might capture memories of her, memories she never got to enjoy with her own mother.

It horrifies me to think about what Mama endured; not long after her diagnosis, she and my father divorced, and she retained custody of me and my sister and brother. Treatments were barbaric 40 years ago, and throughout her illness she underwent five major surgeries, chemotherapy, and radiation.

I have vivid memories of standing at our apartment window that overlooked the parking lot, waiting on her return from the hospital where she often went when the pain was unbearable. She was addicted to pain medication, and my father threatened to take us away if she didn't undergo electric shock therapy, the recommended treatment at the time.

And so she did it…for us.

Upon learning this only in recent years, I remembered that scene from *A Beautiful Mind*, and I cried.

> When we are afraid we ought not to occupy ourselves with endeavoring to prove that there is no danger, but in strengthening ourselves to go on in spite of the danger (Mark Rutherford).

I never recall Mama complaining. I don't remember seeing her cry.

I do remember her telling my sister and me about the birds and the bees, and I remember the day she wrote her will; I think I was flipping over the sofa and my sister was sitting nearby (probably more cognizant of what we were doing), and somehow Mama managed to do this without falling apart.

She did that for us too.

Mama had nine years to train and teach me, shape and guide me; nine years to impress upon me the things most important to her; nine years to brand her legacy.

Watching her then and lingering over a backward gaze through time, I marvel at her courage. I never knew if she was lonely or scared or angry at her circumstances, but I did know she loved us fiercely and her faith sustained her. One of my favorite gifts I received from Mama was my sterling charm bracelet; the most beloved charm, a glass-encased mustard seed, reminded me that a little faith could move mountains.

> The courage of life is often a less dramatic spectacle than the courage of a final moment; but it is no less a magnificent mixture of triumph and tragedy (John F. Kennedy).

Mama died a few months after my brother's fifth birthday, fulfilling her vow and leaving him a collection of memories.

When I think of courage, glimpses of cowardly lions and military heroes come to mind for a moment; yet ultimately, the most courageous person I've ever known is the Steel Magnolia who gave me life and faced her own death with uncommon valor.

I wanted you to see what real courage is...
It's when you know you're licked before you begin
but you begin anyway
and you see it through no matter what. You
rarely win, but sometimes you do.

ATTICUS FINCH,
in Harper Lee's *To Kill a Mockingbird*

27

Like a Single Mother

Kaitlin Curtice

In 2015, my mother came to Atlanta to watch me in a production called *Listen to Your Mother*. At the show I read an essay called "Walking at Sweetwater Creek" about coming alive to my Native American heritage and what it taught me about the women who came before me.

Before the show began, Mom and I went to a nearby coffee shop to spend some time together. We mostly laughed and talked about our journeys, how they brought us to this moment. We talked about how sometimes I listen to my mother and sometimes I don't, but that we're still mother and daughter, still alive to each other, still connected through all these other women who tether us to who we are. We knew that our own family journey hadn't always been easy, but nevertheless, it was *ours*.

When I was nine, my mother became a single mom, left to care for three children under one tiny duplex roof in southern Missouri. I was small then, so I didn't understand all the heaviness that my mother carried. Though I could see weariness in her eyes, a little unsteadiness in her gait, I knew that what was most important was pressing on.

She converted the garage into her bedroom.

She kept us safe and secure.

She let us grow and paced herself in motherhood, even when she was tired.

And I saw Jesus in that.

I was 19 when I got married, and so we entered into the leaving and cleaving stage earlier than some people do.

Leaving and cleaving is hard and steady work, and what I have learned about it is that you get to take what your family gave you and let it send you out to create your own life, to walk your own journey, to love your own family in only the way you know how.

But first, there is the emptying out. That's what she gave me early on as a nine-year-old, as a preteen, as a teenager. The pouring out makes room for the leaving and cleaving, so that it is possible for our dreams to expand beyond us into the realms of God that are beautiful mystery. At times it makes sense, it flows and it's easy, and at times it's hard and the stretching is painful. And yet it is a reflection of the kingdom, of the ebb and flow of our relationship with Jesus, who filled up His own disciples, poured Himself out and into them, and then sent them out.

Jesus said to them, "Go…I am with you always" (Matthew 28:19-20). Every part of this phrase is important, and in the context of relationships between mothers and daughters, it matters so much that the sending off is meant to be an extension of us and then become an extension of the kingdom of God.

So maybe the very first pouring out was at birth, when my mother saw me and said, "You are the future."

Then at age nine, when she was tired and alone, when from her own surviving she said, "You will survive."

And then at 19 when I got married, when she said, "You will leave and cleave."

And then I continue to leave and cleave, and we walk into the calling made for both of us—continuing into the world, and for the rest of my life. And in that, I carry her with me, those pieces. As I create my own identity, I learn how to empty myself out into my own children—the same kind of kenosis through which Jesus first emptied Himself for us.

So the relationship between mothers and daughters truly an extension of Christ's relationship to us, a relationship that sends us out into the world to discover who we are meant to be.

Like a single mother, [Jesus] fed his spiritual offspring from his own flesh and blood until all of his reserves were gone.

BARBARA BROWN TAYLOR

28

Porch Swing Confession

Diane Bailey

Billowy gray fills the southern sky, blowing the hot breath of summer across the lake. Pinecones hit the metal roof, then roll down onto the deck, causing everyone to jump, then laugh.

My daughter and I sit on the porch swing watching the storm roll past with all of its fury.

Lightning crackles as thunder chases the wind. We tuck the old blanket around our hips, as one foot rocks us, keeping rhythm with the song I'm humming softly by The Judds, "Rockin' with the Rhythm of the Rain."

My daughter is my best friend, and I am hers. We have been seated on the first row of many storms of life. Talking things through, at times with a great passion for opposing points of view. We can be brutally honest with each other. At times our words can draw emotional blood, yet we are fierce if anyone else speaks unkindly of the other.

During most of her growing-up life, I was a single mother. She saw how I put her needs before my own, and how hard I had to work to keep a roof over our head. She did her part as she learned to wash clothes and start supper for us. I was her first example of womanhood, showing her how to navigate life, though she has had several mentors other than me as she went through college and then began her career.

A mother is our first mentor, helping us navigate life. Moms are the ones who first teach us to make friends, understand the actions of others, and set the example of a godly woman. Setting a perfect example in front of our children is *not* the most important example we give our daughters. Living authentically in front of them is more important.

Life is not easy or perfect. They need to see the good, but they need us to teach them how to handle their mistakes. And they need to see what to do when a mean girl gossips about them or what to think when life is not fair.

She needs to learn what to do when the coach's daughter is chosen for the All-Stars but she has the better stats. Or when someone talks unkindly about her and she overhears. This is when you can share your stories. Let her know you have been through a similar situation. Let her know how you handled it—even if your response was not ideal.

Laugh and let her know that you might think about putting superglue on the cell phone of a gossip. Then set the example of praying for your enemies and showing kindness when anger kindles.

We want to show our daughters the perfect woman, but they learn so much more when they see how we respond to our brokenness and the brokenness of those around us.

I have yelled, broken promises, used words that should not be used by a mom, forgotten to send money, and been so late she was the last one waiting to be picked up. But in it all, she knew without a doubt she was loved. She knew that no matter where I failed her, I was trying my very best.

God gives the grace needed in parenting when love is the rule. In God's own miraculous way, He is able to use our failures for good. I don't know if I will ever cease to be amazed at the magnitude of His mercy, grace, and redeeming power. He took a child bent on rebellion and a mom soaked in the sorrows of single parenting to create lives for His glory.

Mother and daughter by birth, forever friends by choice.

Heavy rain now pelts the tin roof as her head rests on my shoulder and we gently swing.

There's no way to be a perfect mother
and a million ways to be a good one.

JILL CHURCHILL

29

A Letter to My Daughter

Wendy Dunham

Dear Erin,

Anyone meeting you for the first time would probably never guess what you've been through; wounds aren't always visible. You're one of those people who can walk into a room and make every head turn. At 25, you're beautiful. The funny thing is, I don't think you realize it. Not only are you beautiful outside, you're incredibly beautiful inside as well. Given all you've been through, sometimes I wonder how you turned out so amazing.

I can hardly believe it's been 14 years since our world seemed to fall apart. What started out as an ordinary day for you as an 11-year-old ended in a tragedy that altered our lives. You'd woken up that morning, hopped on the school bus, and gone to school as usual. And like any other weekday, I went to work.

Being a latchkey child, you returned home from school that day expecting to wait for your brother to come home. Your father's truck was in the driveway—normally Dad wasn't home from work yet. Seeing his truck, you ran into the house to find him. What you found, however, was something no 11-year-old child should ever have to see.

Your daddy—the man who was meant to be your protector—was in the living room, overdosed, with his wrist cut in an attempt to end his life. What he didn't realize was that his attempt to end his life would not work, but rather would end his relationship with you. We've learned that people who suffer from untreated mental illness don't always see things clearly.

Soon after that day you developed anorexia, which isn't surprising for a young girl after experiencing a traumatic event. I did all I could to help, but it wasn't enough to keep you from being hospitalized. To this day I'm not sure you've fully forgiven me for having to take you to the eating disorder's unit at the hospital and having to leave you there. It was one of the most difficult things I've ever done. But I had to do it. It was a matter of choosing life for you.

We've also learned that anorexia can be a long journey. After your hospital stay, you went to several step-down programs before finally coming back home. And then as part of your ongoing treatment program, you and I had to plan meals and grocery shop together, which was no easy feat. And being the one responsible for your calorie intake, the one making you eat and fighting against the resistance of anorexia, I felt like I was driving a wedge between us while at the same time fighting for your life.

Not long afterward I noticed scars on your arms; you'd begun harming yourself another way. But I knew that the heart-wrenching pain I felt as your mother was likely nothing in comparison to the pain you were trying to manage. I took you to so many counseling appointments, but since you weren't ready to receive help, counseling seemed futile.

But one thing helped—the summer camp you went to. While there, you made friends, you learned about God, and you were taken under the wing of a godly camp counselor who mentored you for many years. That was just one of the many blessings that God had in store.

You've always loved to dance, which is why I signed you up for your first dance class when you were only four. You continued dancing for years, as if it breathed life into your soul. You seemed at your happiest when you were dancing. But at some point it seemed to become a two-edged sword—one edge was a form of healthy self-expression, and the other, sharp and jagged, which battled your body image. You continued dancing your way into high school, but as you reached the end of your junior year, you'd developed friendships I felt were unhealthy. When I realized a shift was needed, I arranged for you to change dance schools and high schools come your senior year, both Christian-based. Although it was difficult at the time, I'm thankful you now look back and say it was a good decision.

Even with those changes, you continued to struggle. We both knew that as the single mom I'd become, I couldn't provide you with the type of family I longed for you to experience. So when God opened doors for you to temporarily live with a Christian family—one that had at its center a healthy Christian marriage—I knew it was another one of God's blessings. Although I was grateful for the opportunity, I struggled with feeling like I'd failed you.

Now, several years later, God has continued blessing you by providing you with an amazing job opportunity where you are flourishing. I can't help but smile as I think of how faithful God has been.

Aside from your employment, you're currently at a time in your life when God has given you a blank slate. You have choices to make. My role as your mother is to continue loving you, praying for you, and trusting that God will give you wisdom in every choice you make.

Looking back over our journey, although I still feel that painful ache that comes as part of tragedy, I am happy as I look forward to your future. And the most important thing I've learned, and one I hope you realize as well, is that your heavenly Father is always one step ahead. He makes the way clear and provides for your specific needs. And although you are incredibly loved, adored, and cherished by me, I know that the One who holds you in the palm of His hands loves you even more.

And by the way, would you have ever imagined you'd be teaching dance at that very same Christian-based dance school, and that you would have developed such wonderful relationships there? Our God is amazing. I hope you never forget.

And lastly, Erin, if you ever feel alone or think you've lost your way, remember to remember…sometimes it's only in looking back that we can smile at our future.

I'll love you for always,
Mom

"I know the plans I have for you," declares the Lord,
"plans to prosper you and not to harm you,
plans to give you hope and a future."

JEREMIAH 29:11 NIV

Part 6

Quality Time

To every thing there is a season, and a time to every purpose under the heaven.

ECCLESIASTES 3:1

30

The Power of One

Krista Gilbert

Ice cubes jostled back and forth through the bubbles as my daughter stirred her drink with one hand. Frustrated, I sat back in my chair and folded my arms. This was a special weekend away, just the two of us! Why was she so far away?

There had been a time when she was my sidekick. If I was cooking, she was next to me sautéing, mixing, or tasting. If I was gardening, she was right there picking flowers or pointing out ladybugs to her younger brother. If I was exercising, she was doing "push-ups" right next to me. But then one day she began to hang around a little less, and then after getting a phone, even less, until my sidekick was nowhere to be found.

I knew the tumultuous waters she was navigating as a young teenager, and I wanted to be there for her, but I felt like she kept pushing me out of the boat. The temptation to swim away in retreat, hurt and anger was great, but I knew that wasn't the answer.

So there we sat, in awkward silence, eating our Italian meatballs and spaghetti.

The next morning I woke up with renewed energy. "Good morning, sunshine!" I pulled the pillow off her head. A soft smile crept up the corners of her face. The mention of the French bakery down the street was all it took to get her tired body out of bed. By the time we rode the elevator in white bathrobes and landed in the swimming pool that afternoon, we were doing handstand contests in the pool and striking poses for selfies. The walls had come down. The essence of my girl, not so little anymore, was back. In less than 24 hours, her spirit with me had undergone a complete transformation.

The teen years are complicated. Sometimes your kids draw you in, and other times they push you away. But this truth comes back to me again and again: more than ever they need parents who consistently show up and never stop trying to build the relationship. They need to know that the most foundational relationships in their life are strong enough to hold their emotional weight.

At the end of that weekend I kept asking myself, "Why do I forget the power of spending one-on-one time with my child?" When we walked back into the door of our home, our hearts were once again reconnected and soft toward one another, and that was worth every penny spent on a hotel room and every ounce of planning it took to make the time away happen.

In relationships we have to keep getting to know the people we love, *in present tense*. While many aspects of our children's personalities do not change, as they grow, they emerge more fully into who they are becoming. Spending individual time with them helps us get to know who that emerging person is, and connects us to them in a way that is difficult to do when you are with other people. As I look back over our parenting years thus far, there are many things we could have done differently, but the one practice that has positively impacted our relationships with our children more than any other is spending one-on-one time with them. And I will eat spaghetti and meatballs for the rest of my life if it means that my heart gets to stay connected to theirs.

At the end of your life, you will never regret not having passed one more test, not winning one more verdict, or not closing one more deal. You will regret time not spent with a husband, a friend, a child, or a parent.

BARBARA BUSH

31

I See You

Elizabeth Maxon

I was tired. A week of fighting fevers and sniffles will do that to you. When tiny bodies aren't healthy, my heart and mind can fail me too. My task list had grown too long and my patience too short.

"Eyeballs! Lucy, I am talking to you. I need to see your eyes looking in my eyes!"

Crossed arms, scowling four-year-old face, boring a hole through the floor to avoid my gaze.

Finally, they wander up to mine. Those beautiful eyes, cool blue one moment and warm green the next. Their color changes, and so does their message.

In that moment they were hardened. They were shutting me out. They were telling me I was not welcome. They were speaking of anger and shame and wanting to be left alone. They were tiny but impenetrable walls of protection. For a moment I looked at them with contempt because they were keeping me from the place I was trying to get to. They were keeping me from her heart.

In an instant I remembered all the other precious messages those eyes had sent me over the years and I softened.

In those moments when I need her to see me, to hear me, I get so frustrated. How can I make her see? What she said was hurtful. How she behaved was unkind. Can't she see that I'm only trying to teach her? Why won't she let my eyes meet hers so we can see each other?

And then I was stopped short by different questions: How are my eyes reacting to hers? What message are my eyes sending?

Yes, I was tired. Yes, I'd had the "eyeball" talk with her one too many times, but I knew I needed to make some behavior changes if I was going to expect any out of her.

We had spun webs of arguments that ended with her little words packing big punches...

"I am super sad you are not playing this with me right now."

"I went upstairs because I was so upset that you wouldn't get me a straw."

"You are so mean...I will never do that!"

"Sometimes I get so mad I wish you would leave me alone!"

I'm not kidding. At four years old she said those things. Sometimes I wish I could be so honest instead of giving someone the silent treatment for two days. There is no passive-aggressive business with my girl. She can articulate her emotions and express them a million different ways.

When she asked me to go play in the backyard, I was in the middle of getting some things done and I really didn't want to go. It was cold. I had work to do. And—you probably take this part for granted—I was *tired.*

Then this thought. This flying-out-of-nowhere, slam-my-back-up-against-the-wall thought. *Eyeballs! She needs to see your eyes looking in her eyes.*

I shut my laptop and my gaze meets hers. There they were, like an invitation. Full of anticipation. Full of hope. Full of love. I grabbed her hand and we walked down the steps, across the yard, and onto the trampoline. We jumped and we laughed and we tickled and we talked. We saw each other.

My mind was so full with this one thought: *Your eyes will need to meet softly this way millions of times so they can ultimately stand up to the hard, glaring meetings ahead.* If our eyes don't meet when she is twirling around the kitchen in her princess dress, or when she wants to do an art project, or when she is trying to scramble eggs all by herself, or when she just found the coolest worm ever on the sidewalk, or when she is flying high above the trampoline—if our eyes never see each other in those momentary joy-filled, life-giving, carefree moments—how will they ever face the other ones? The ones that come on the tail of a big mistake, a moment of fear, a weakness to peer pressure, a loss of control, a fall from grace, a broken heart?

I know those heavy moments will come. This child whose wild self still fits onto my hip will grow. She will become too big for me to carry, too old for me to cuddle, too busy for me to rock, but I won't give up her eyes. I will fight to hold their gaze. I will lock onto them in all the moments she offers them because I know there will be days when seeing each other will be a battle. It's a battle we must win.

I see you, my sweet girl. I see you.

Lord, purge our eyes to see
Within the seed a tree
Within the glowing egg a bird
Within the shroud a butterfly.
Till taught by such we see
Beyond all creatures, Thee...

CHRISTINA ROSSETTI

32

My Daughter

Adrian Wood

My daughter falls between three brothers. She is resolute. She is efficient and proactive, a smaller and sweeter version of myself. Her gap-toothed smile stares back at me in my old school pictures. She longs for my time, and so often I tell her that I am unavailable before six thirty in the morning, but not today.

I stayed up too late last night, so I had groggily made my way downstairs to make a cup of Folger's and slowly wake up in the 30 minutes of quiet darkness that I claim on school days. Nope. Not today. Not on this cold and still-dark Friday morning of November.

There she stands, a messy-haired sprite, dressed in a pink T-shirt and some nautical-looking summer pants. I can't tell her to go put on real pants as I know there are none in her bottom drawer. No, it is still filled with shorts, as I have yet to unpack the winter clothes, and the few things she does have out for cold mornings are still in the dryer from last evening.

We put a Band-Aid on her mosquito bite (or maybe a mean spider bite) that she thinks happened in her bed last night or on the playground. I make coffee for me and hot cocoa for her; my ready agreement to this splurge before breakfast brings a screech of giddiness.

What a mother can learn in 30 minutes.

I hear about the boy in her class who was suspended for a week and listen to some of his really bad words, like *fart.* I sign her folder and reading log after being asked only one time and carefully examine each sheet she unearths proudly from her backpack.

I sit and she talks and I put her flower girl bracelet on and of course do it wrong. I agree to painting her toes tonight, even though I don't own any polish. Yes, I tell her, we can sleep in my bed since Daddy and the big boys will be away. I smile to myself thinking of the tiny girl who has arms and legs like a writhing orangutan and prefers to ask questions rather than count sheep.

This seven-year-old daughter of mine is quite fetching, and to be moved by her very presence is a gift that I have missed too often, but not today. Someday the quiet mornings will come in a forever set of waves, and I will drink hot coffee and I will miss her and the little body that once clambered for my lap. I will close my eyes in those years to come, thinking of the girl for whom I chose to abandon my dreams of quiet for the love that I hoped would reach far beyond those simple mornings.

Let me love you a little more, before you're not little anymore.

ANONYMOUS

33

No Regrets

Elisa Pulliam

One would think that navigating through the rain and heavy traffic to make it to a doctor's appointment wouldn't exactly be the ideal setting for a meaningful time between a mother and daughter. But it was priceless, because in a few months, she'd be flying from our nest, heading off to college. Time has gone too fast for this mama's heart.

As we gently wrestled our hands into the trail mix, giggling at our effort to stave off hunger pains and stay focused on directions, Leah confessed the sweetest words: "Mom, this is just like when you homeschooled me. It was the best year of my whole life. I loved spending that time with you."

Oh my, the Lord is indeed kind. I had no idea what fruit would come from that sacrifice of time and that great adventure. When we decided to homeschool Leah, the goal was to give her everything she needed to launch into adulthood. She excelled academically, but seemed to lack the skills necessary for caring for herself, her home, and a family in the future. Probably typical for a twelve-year-old, but seeing as we lived in a boarding-school community, she wasn't quite keeping up with her peers, who managed to fly in from all over the world, keep up with their studies, and even do their own laundry. My bent toward thinking long-term made me concerned for Leah's future, and my commitment to the mission of motherhood made me willing (by the grace of God) to lay down my career and ministry to devote time to her needs.

So that homeschool year was all about mentoring Leah in matters of the heart, soul, and home. She learned how to balance a budget, grocery shop, cook, plan a holiday gathering, set up a guest room, and cultivate a quiet time. I wanted this precious oldest daughter of mine to become a woman who could steward her giftings, responsibilities, and resources for the glory of God. Yes, quite a lofty goal, but this was my first go-around. I prayed that this priceless season together would enable me to shape her faith, influence her heart, and remind her of Whose she was after some difficult years with her elementary school peers.

God kindly answered our prayers for Leah, as that little girl is now all grown up and seriously ready to fly. She's my right hand in so many ways in managing the rhythms of our family routine. She's definitely the best chef in the house, and she shops without ever going over budget. She manages her own responsibilities with incredible attention to detail, all the while moving through social situations with character and conviction that come straight from the Lord.

But the only reason she enjoyed that time with me, and grew into the woman she is now, is entirely because of the grace of God. In the years leading up to our homeschooling time, God orchestrated a bazillion circumstances in my personal life to bring me to terms with the wounds in my heart. Those wounds caused me to be quite the wretch of a mother. I was short-tempered and often yelled like a banshee. I was overly critical and harsh. But through the challenge of my husband, the encouragement of a dear friend, the support of a counselor, and the strength of the Lord, I got the help I needed to deal with the pain stored up in my heart from a childhood filled with abuse and from the guilt over so many damaging choices. God met me in my brokenness. He graciously bathed me in His forgiveness and truth and deactivated the bomb hidden in my heart with His love and grace. He changed me from the inside out, and made me into the mentor mom I always wanted to be.

God healed me and equipped me to invest into my daughter's story for His glory.

It wasn't about homeschooling or budgeting, grocery shopping or having a quiet time. Yes, God answered my prayers for her to learn the practical skills she needed to launch into adulthood. But more importantly, He shaped my daughter's heart and life through His redemptive work not only in me but also in our relationship. He chose to use me as one of her greatest influences, as He flowed through me freely with His love and grace. Without the healing He did on my heart, I can't imagine where our relationship would be today. It's that work that makes me confident she is ready to fly our nest, because she knows full well God changes people. He redeems a mess. He changes a legacy. And He is trustworthy to bring to completion the good work He began in all of us. It's because she knows Whose she is, and who she is, that I can watch her fly with no regret.

The art of mothering is to teach
the art of living to children.

ELAINE HEFFNER

34

The Letters Between Us

Jennifer Dukes Lee

Dear Daughter,

You brushed up against me in the kitchen last night when you were browning hamburger and I was chopping garden radishes.

Right then I remembered all the times we've melted into each other over your 11 years on earth: in the nursery rocker; nestled in your tiny hospital bed that week when you were so sick; in a dark movie theater when our hands reached for the same box of Milk Duds; on a shore in Haiti with our legs stretched out together while we watched the moon rise over the sea; countless nights under your quilt, debating who loved who more. (All the way to Jupiter and back, babe.)

You always seemed so small next to me.

But now? I turned around, and you were this little woman at the stove, stirring. The steam rose from a boiling pot on the stovetop; you swiped your forehead with the back of your hand.

I blinked my eyes, and that's how fast you traveled from *Goodnight Moon* to *Good Luck Charlie* to good home cooking in our kitchen. Good gracious, girl, you've grown up.

You asked for the salt, and your voice was so small, and I think that's God's way of making this growing-up thing easier on a mama. He's kept your voice little, to let me know that you're still my baby. I handed you the salt shaker, and I kept my mouth shut, because you might have rolled your eyes if I said then what I'm going to tell you now:

Daughter, I hope you'll never get too old to ask me for something. It won't always be for the salt, or for me to turn the light back on, or to scratch your back. But I hope you'll never stop asking for a bit of advice. For another prayer.

I wonder if you'll remember too much of what I did wrong. That's one of a parent's worst fears, you know. That her child will grow up remembering the awful parts—those times when we raised our voice too loud, set our jaw too hard. I'd be devastated if the worst moments drowned out the best ones.

Daughter, I hope that you've heard, above all else, the love. I pray that my heart spoke loudest.

I also pray this: In a world where people are unfriended with the click of a mouse, I hope you know you'll never get de-loved in this house. You're loved because of who you are, not because of what grade you get, what college accepts you, what job you land.

And if you ever want to know for sure? Come back and slip your sweet self next to me, like you did when I held you in my arms, when I rocked you in the nursing chair, when we made supper in a hot Iowa kitchen on a night in July. I'll tell you, again and again until I can't tell you any more, that you can trust in God's love, and you can also trust in mine.

Love,
Mom

P.S. I love you to Jupiter and back—times fifty!

—

Dear Mom,

Let me ease your worries. We all make mistakes. I don't remember the mistakes we've *both* made because I think the good of this world always surpasses the bad.

I remember you for the chocolate chip waffles and peanut butter toast.

For the prayers before bed.

For the times you came to my soccer games to cheer me on.

For help with sheep chores in the morning.

For studying with me for all those extra-hard science tests.

Let me sum it all up in five words: for the love you give.

As your daughter, I expect things from you. I look to you for comfort and encouragement. If I'm sad or just need to talk, you're my go-to girl.

In your letter to me, you talked about sharing space. Just a few minutes ago we were in the garden. I was pulling weeds, and you were harvesting lettuce. I love to work together with you like that. I held up my hands, caked in dirt. You held out the hose, and I rinsed off my hands in the ice-cold water. Then you aimed the hose at my mud-splattered feet. I let out a shriek, and we both laughed.

These are moments I will treasure forever.

You love me—the me with all my quirks. The me who loves to randomly break into song. And you know the verses to all my silly songs. You love the me who once nearly liquefied a Pop-Tart in the microwave. (Hey, how was I supposed to know it only needed to be in there for 15 seconds—not 3 minutes?)

So, thank you, Mom. For everything.

Love,
Lydia

P.S. Jupiter? That's so lame. I love you to *Saturn* and back—times infinity.

Yours is the light by which my spirit's born...
you are my sun, my moon, and all my stars.

E.E. CUMMINGS

35

Taking Wing

Lynn D. Morrissey

It was late spring, and my young daughter, Sheridan, and I decided to plan some special mother-daughter activities to share. With a little trepidation, I allowed her to adopt a caterpillar at a local birdseed store as one way to make a memory.

Sheridan, notorious for collecting crawling critters that always made *my* skin crawl, brought home her undulating invertebrate in a covered plastic cup. Gingerly placing the striped caterpillar she'd dubbed Sunrise in a darkened corner of our kitchen, Sheridan promised to feed her, tend her, and keep her at a respectable distance from me. Though never fond of things that creep, I was still fascinated by the assurance that this tiny insect would soon morph into a big, beautiful butterfly. I could hardly wait to share this experience with my daughter.

Daily I watched as Sheridan emptied the cup of the mostly eaten milkweed leaves she had inserted the night before, careful not to cast away her insect gourmand in the process. I was surprised at the creature's ravenous appetite, and even more astounded by its exponential growth. Each day Sunrise seemed to triple her girth and length. To accommodate her weight gain, on several occasions she shed her skin like a too-tight pair of panty hose, shimmying out of it one wiggle at a time.

One momentous morning Sunrise crawled to the lid of the cup, tenaciously attached herself, and shed her skin one last time. And then, in the stillness of that magical moment, she revealed a chrysalis of shimmering green and unseen dreams. And she waited.

So did we.

Over the ensuing days, Sheridan and I shared our hopes for the small tenant residing inside the chrysalis. And in the process, Sheridan tentatively began sharing her *own* hopes and dreams with me as she shimmied out of her childhood one wobbly wiggle at a time—encouraged by the promise of Sunrise's metamorphosis.

Then one day, in the fullness of time, in the fullness of a promise realized, we beheld a brilliant butterfly, her orange-and-black stained glass wings trembling inside the cup. As she began to pump and fill her wings, we too trembled at her breathtaking beauty *and* at the thought of letting her go. Mustering our courage, we took Sunrise to the garden to free her, praying she'd linger among the lilacs a while. She circled slowly above the purple petals, then suddenly flew to the treetops. Alighting for just an instant, she fluttered her wings like little rays of sunshine flashing on black branches. Then she ascended higher still and finally disappeared from our sight.

Sheridan and I decided to adopt a new caterpillar every spring and raise it together. And I promised myself that I would nurture my own little butterfly whose childhood was flitting away with great speed—and that one day I would love her enough to let her take wing, just as we had done for Sunrise.

When I made that promise, I fully intended to keep it. But in an unexpected twist that only the Lord could have orchestrated, I have come to understand over the years that it truly has been Sheridan who has nurtured *me.* Despite my shaky start as her mother and my mistakes along the way, Sheridan has indeed taken wing, encouraging me to rise right along with her. Without her faithful example, I'd still be crawling like a caterpillar.

I didn't gracefully surrender to motherhood. As a full-time career woman who encountered a surprise pregnancy at forty, I was filled with fear and resentment, fighting God's will. And even after I accepted

God's plan for my daughter and me, I usually found myself flying by the seat of my parental panty hose, shimmying awkwardly around one wobbly wiggle at a time, trying to find a comfortable fit for motherhood. I had no idea what I was doing.

But as my beautiful, gentle daughter and I shared our lives—walking, talking, and tea partying through our years together—God softened my heart. As I began to shed my lethargy, I filled my wings with Sheridan's energy; my rebellion with her joy; my cynicism with her optimism; my jadedness with her innocence; my workaholism with her play. I grew mentally and emotionally as she and I explored her world, and spiritually as I taught her about God.

And while I may have taught her about the Lord chapter and verse from the Bible, as Sheridan continued to grow to maturity, it was she who taught me how to love Him with all my heart and to honor Him through obedience.

Two examples spring to mind.

One afternoon, when I picked up Sheridan from her high school, I noticed she was uncharacteristically quiet on our drive home. Finally responding to my coaxing, her eyes downcast, she whispered, "Mama, I left my Bible class today. Our teacher showed a movie, and five minutes into it, I told him privately that you wouldn't want me to watch something like that. I told him I needed to wait outside the classroom until the end of the period."

And then she had quietly left the room and sat outside the door.

I was stunned. My shy, gentle girl had graciously confronted her Bible teacher, refusing to watch an indecent movie for what he later told me he had shown for the "sake of discussion." Sheridan's uncompromising resolve prompted me not just to face her teacher, but eventually her principal and school board in what would become a two-year dialogue. I have always retreated from making waves. But because Sheridan had taken a principled stand for morality, her courage gave me the strength to do so too. I rose to the challenge, and her school removed those movies from the curricula.

Later, when Sheridan entered college, she infused me with far greater courage to confront a prejudice I didn't even know I harbored.

She attended a university with a widely diverse student body and easily made friends with students from other countries. She particularly wanted me to meet her most special friend—a young Muslim man from Saudi Arabia. I have always loved meeting Sheridan's friends, but rather than inviting him to our home (as I normally would have), I suggested we meet him in a restaurant for dinner. My reaction surprised me.

As the time for our dinner approached, I knew that I was afraid to meet him—afraid of communicating with someone of another race, fluent in a strange language, of someone with radically different ideologies and religious views. But down deep, I sensed I was terrified of terrorism. I had listened to provocative news reports and feared for Sheridan's safety. I trusted exaggerated perspectives and worst-case scenarios rather than my daughter's own sound judgment and personal knowledge of this boy.

I never revealed my fears to Sheridan before we met her friend that evening. Surprisingly, as we chatted over dinner, I discovered that there was nothing remotely radical about Abdul (as I will call him). He was caring and congenial, loquacious and interesting, sharing in perfect, rapid-fire English about his life back home and how much he missed his mother. He even called her during our dinner, animatedly conversing about our family in his native Arabic.

We shared more in common than what might have separated us—our love for laughter, our love for family, our respect for older people, our love for good literature, our devotion to prayer. In an unguarded moment, he told us that his aunt, who lived in Lebanon, was in constant danger of losing her life. His tears brimmed, and so did mine. My fears had been irrational, but his were real.

Rising to the occasion, wanting our time together to continue in a more personal way, I invited Abdul to our home for dessert. After eating, we retired to the music room where he sang an exquisite song a cappella. As his lyricism calligraphed the air in his native tongue, a kind of foreign filigree, a delicate scrollwork of sound, our hearts soared in its beauty—beauty that transcended nationality and cultural differences. Had I not followed Sheridan's loving, openhearted example, I would have missed the opportunity to offer welcoming hospitality to this precious young man.

Time and again throughout the years, I've realized it's not ultimately I who have raised Sheridan to maturity, but she who has raised me—helping me rise higher still to nobler heights above my self-centeredness, inadequacy, and fear. And through her continued kindness and patience, encouraging me to become the best mother I can be, through her waiting on the fullness of a promise realized, Sheridan has loved me enough to help me take wing.

Well, I must endure the presence of a
few caterpillars if I wish to become
acquainted with the butterflies.

ANTOINE DE SAINT-EXUPÉRY,
The Little Prince

Part 7

Teachable Moments

When you know better, you do better.

MAYA ANGELOU

36

Dressing Room Discovery

Elizabeth Foss

I'm certain I've been dreading this event since before she was born. Beautiful girl child of mine—my little dash of femininity wedged between five boys. She has grown into a young woman, curves appearing where once there were straight lines. And now it is time to go find clothes to fit the new figure.

Before we go, we are blessed to spend a Saturday afternoon at a mother-daughter tea at our church. A fashion expert entertains the ladies there and also offers insight about what to wear. Listening to her and participating in the quizzes and conversation, my daughter and I learn some valuable lessons about each other. I'm made very aware of her color and style preferences. She is made aware of appropriateness and the "fun" factor of wearing just the right thing. We both leave a little more enlightened and a lot more enthusiastic about the task ahead of us.

So nervous am I that I drive two hours west to a familiar college town. Perhaps it will be easier here where the salespeople are likely to be more helpful and less brusque than in my busy city. My stepmother comes along to offer moral support and a sense of style. We can do this.

Darling, beautiful daughter gathers an armful of promising fashions into her arms, trying to find things similar to those she saw at the tea. She tries one on. And then another. And then another. I see the storm gathering in her eyes, threatening to spill onto her cheeks. There is darkening where once the thrill of anticipation glowed.

"What? What is it?" I cry, panic rising in my throat.

"It's me," she says. "I look terrible in everything. I wanted to buy beautiful things. I wanted this to be fun. But I look terrible in everything."

I leave her there in front of that indicting mirror. A thousand dressing room mirrors from a thousand similar outings come back to haunt me. I hear it as if it were yesterday. "You're too short. Too much tummy. Too much bust. Not enough leg."

I look desperately at my stepmother. I so don't want this trip to go into that all-too-familiar territory. I'm praying now. I want to understand it all. All I can say is, "I don't want her to be like me. I want her to love the way she looks."

Barbara is relaxed and positive. "She's beautiful."

And that's all she says. And with those words, I understand. Of course she's beautiful. She's fresh and unadulterated. She's exactly as God intended. It's not about her.

And it was never about me.

I walk back into the dressing room and speak with a certainty I do not yet believe. "Get dressed. We're going to a different store. These clothes are poorly made. They're cut skimpily from cheap fabric for fashion models who starve themselves. They're not made for real, healthy young women."

She takes a deep breath and follows me into the mall, fighting tears. I pray my way into another store and there we begin to pull more appropriate clothing from the racks. I'm relieved to find that though we have come to a more expensive store, the sales are blessing us. My beautiful child finds clothing that suits her perfectly. She beams from the dressing room.

When our mission is complete and we've returned home, I turn to the man who's loved me since I was her age. I tell him about that moment in the dressing room when I recognized how easy it would have been for our daughter to have had a distorted sense of herself. He knows about all my dressing room days. He is quiet, waiting for me to come to a full understanding. And finally, finally, I see myself as he has seen me all these years.

Why take ye thought for raiment?
Consider the lilies of the field, how they grow;
they toil not, neither do they spin: And yet I
say unto you, That even Solomon in all his
glory was not arrayed like one of these.

MATTHEW 6:28-29

37

Daughter, Dear

Dawn Camp

Dear Sabra,

You're my oldest girl, the one I wondered if we'd ever have after starting with your three older brothers. You came into the world with the round face, big cheeks, and little mouth of a Cabbage Patch doll. Nurses commented on the likeness in the delivery room and parents stopped to point you out to their kids in the grocery store. You live dramatically, and your entrance wasn't any different: cord wrapped around your neck so tight the doctor had to cut it loose mid-delivery. From day one you've been your daddy's little princess; it's the right of a firstborn daughter.

You've always been talkative with those you know but shy with those you don't. Remember your kindergarten graduation? You were the only child who wouldn't go onstage to get your diploma; Miss Karen and I had to take it to you in the audience. You wouldn't order fast food for yourself, and also said a firm no to dental X-rays and stitches. You finally had to agree to the stitches when you wrecked your scooter and split your chin wide open at the Labor Day church picnic when you were six.

You were our resident hairdresser and would spend as long as it took to fix one of the other girls' hair, even if it meant there was no time to fix your own. You have patience and talent for it, and maybe someday you'll pursue it as a career. I'll never forget when you picked up the clippers at a friend's house and buzzed off your bangs in a straight (if not horizontal) line just below the hairline. And we had church directory pictures that week! I tried to tuck your itty-bitty bangs beneath a headband and hoped people would notice your smile instead of your hair-cutting experiment.

You've always been a champion of the underdog, your daddy's viewing partner for those sci-fi B movies that you both enjoy, and our resident Shakespearen scholar. How many times have you read *Romeo and Juliet*? People are drawn to you and you are truly an original. Yours can be an incredibly powerful testimony.

Your teen years were hard on us both. My mother always said, "You're only as happy as your least happy child," and there were days, maybe years, when joy was hidden like four-leaf clovers among the weeds. We share a middle name, but there were days I wondered if we shared much else. You lived your own way and wrote your own rules and shunned my advice more than you embraced it, but the years have softened us both and we're growing into the relationship I always hoped we'd have.

Now you're married and expecting a child! They say every mother wants her daughter to have a daughter of her own, and I see that it's true. In my mind you carry a baby girl who will share our middle name. I pray this little one heals broken places in your soul in the way only a child can. You've become a stronger person, more intentional about taking care of yourself, because your body shelters another life. You're learning the fierce, protective love a mother holds for something—for *someone*—she's never seen.

A few months from now I'll hand you a book and point out this story, *your* story, to read (after you pass me my new grandbaby, of course). By then you'll have experienced that first heady taste of motherhood and I imagine you'll be sleep deprived but happy. Remember, Princess, I'm always here for you.

Love,
Mom

We struggle to accept that our children's destinies are not ours to write,their battles not ours to fight, their bruises not ours to bear, nor their victories ours to take credit for. We learn humility and how to ask for help.We learn to let go even when every fiber of our being yearns to hold on even tighter.

KATRINA KENISON,

Magical Journey: An Apprenticeship in Contentment

38

Dressed with Salvation

Amanda White

She was only three years old and a new big sister. Her face was so tiny, like a little mouse. Her hair soft, her voice sweet. She was wearing pink fairy pajamas. We were waking up slowly, watching *Sesame Street* during breakfast. It was always my favorite time of the day—just the two of us awake and rambling around the house.

After breakfast, I curled on the couch to find some phone numbers on the computer while she sat on the floor crafting. She had pieces of felt and bits of yarn, plus a pair of little kid scissors. I loved watching her create and treasured the fact she was doing it at my feet, wanting to be near me.

I got on the phone while she continued to make her special creation. I could see she had started moving around, laying on the ground and getting back up, wiggling like a fish out of water.

When I hung up the phone she was on me in a flash. "I want to change clothes!" But it wasn't the can-I-wear-my-Snow-White-dress kind of request, more of an I-need-to-go-potty demand. I wasn't fazed and told her that we would when I was done, that I still had more phone calls to make.

A few moments later she started jumping up and down, demanding, "I want to change clothes! I want to change clothes!" I was totally oblivious to the depth of her concern and was about to shoo her away again when she suddenly blurted, "I am hiding something from you! I am hiding something from you!"

My heart lurched. What could my precious little girl be hiding? We have been sitting next to each other for the last hour. My mind was not catching up with my daughter's emotions.

Then I looked down and saw her little hand covering a part of her pajamas. Did she accidentally go potty? But then it clicked. Those scissors! "Did you cut a hole in your pants?"

Her sweet, tiny face dropped. Tears filled her eyes, and she nodded at me.

"Is that why you were moving around and lying on the floor? Is that why you asked if you could change clothes?"

She nodded again.

I pulled this petite little girl into my arms and spoke softly, "Do you know the two things you did wrong? You purposely used those scissors on your pants, which you know not to do. We only cut paper, remember? And then you hid it from Mommy. Do you know what that's called?"

Her wide eyes stared at me.

"It's a lie. A lie makes Jesus sad. It makes Mommy sad too."

Now it had made her sad. Her face wasn't defiant at getting caught, or mad because she was about to get in trouble, but oh-so-sad she had done it. Contrition was laced in every tear.

And my mind? Reeling, because I didn't know what to do with a preschooler who was contrite over sin! I didn't know how to discipline that little sprite of a thing when she was just so ridiculously adorable!

Surely it would have been appropriate to just say, "Well, don't do it again," and hug it out. But I felt like I couldn't let this opportune moment pass.

We had been memorizing Scriptures for each letter of the alphabet and our *F* verse was, "He forgives all my sins" (Psalm 103:3 NLT). I reminded her of that verse and led her in a prayer asking Jesus to forgive her. She couldn't voice it herself, so I tried to lead her the best I could.

Still, this entire time I was like the emoji with big hearts in my eyes because she was just so cute even in her sorrow. I was frantically wondering how and if I should punish her.

So I told her she'd have to wear the pajamas all day until it was time to go out later. She exploded in tears. Pointing to the hole in her pants she sobbed, "I don't want to wear *these*!"

My heart couldn't take it. I couldn't leave her in those clothes. I stood up, took her hand, and walked her over to the trash can. We pulled off those pajamas and threw them in the trash, and I told her that just as we were throwing away the object of her sin, Jesus threw away our sins when He died on the cross.

That is the day my daughter and I learned about forgiveness. Her repentance, contrition, and godly sorrow were an example to me. It also gave me a little glimpse of how our heavenly Father must feel toward me when I sin. I could only see love when I looked at my daughter, not sin. I only felt sorrow for her pain, not offense at her actions. The prophet Isaiah wrote that God clothes us in "the garments of salvation" and puts robes "of righteousness" on us (61:10). He doesn't want us to live in holey, sinful fairy pajamas, but throws our sins away and looks at us with love!

The people of Jerusalem will say,
"We take great delight in the LORD.
We are joyful because we belong to our God.
He has dressed us with salvation as if it were our clothes.
He has put robes of godliness on us.
We are like a groom who is dressed up for his wedding.
We are like a bride who decorates herself with her jewels."

ISAIAH 61:10 NIRV

39

Give Your Child Every Thing They Want

(and the World Will Lose the Gift of Gratitude)

September McCarthy

Straight from the toaster and onto the delicate plate. Two slices of bread, buttered to the edges and sprinkled with cinnamon and sugar. An even dusting across the top and then neatly stacked to line up the edges. This is where we would get fancy. As fancy as cinnamon toast goes.

With careful and loving precision, my mom took the butter knife straight down through the sugar and the crusts. Straight lines into thin wedges. Still neatly stacked and warm. Served delicately and lovingly with ginger ale, ice, and a straw. The carbonated bubbles minus the caffeine and the cinnamon and sugar ran straight into my senses and still bring memories of comfort and simplicity.

When the other girls had the cutest new tennis shoes and my brothers watched the boys in the neighborhood come home from school to the newest action figures or a long-wished-for baseball glove, my mom would tell us this: "If I gave you everything in life now, then what would you have to look forward to?"

What we were greeted with when she picked us up from school was a paper bag that we could see on the front seat of the car next to her as we all rode along quietly, pretending we knew nothing of its contents. As soon as the car was parked in the driveway, she would hold up the bag and tell us that we could reach inside but not to look. We could feel around and choose a treat, but there was to be no peeking.

I always moved my fingers around the edges of each one, seeing the details in my mind.

Each and every time I pulled out the peanut butter cup. And with their hand deep in the bag, my brothers would find their favorite, and whatever they pulled out, they were over the moon about.

Growing up with gratitude prepared me to remember that even if I had everything I wanted, it would never be enough. Because the gift would soon be gone. The generations will never understand this. Unless we teach them.

Every day I pray that my own children will understand the waiting and the knowing that life is more than things and wanting things. That the simplicities we celebrate are bathed in gratitude for the gifts that God Himself has given us.

We must learn to be thankful together.

For this world is full of wealth and wars against itself in greed. Moth and rust do corrupt.

The simplicity of life has been lost on the bigger and best, and children are raised with bribery. Bribery for behavior.

Do not hand your child life on a silver platter. Allow them to wait and work for the end goal.

You desire to give your child a gift today? Teach them to be thankful for what they have and to not focus on everything they want.

For today, I will serve my own children warm slices of cinnamon toast, cut into slivers. Giving them everything they need in the right time, because their hearts are learning the true meaning of gratefulness. And every day I hear, "Thank you, Mom."

In every thing give thanks: for this is the will of God in Christ Jesus concerning you.

1 THESSALONIANS 5:18

40

Belly Button Love

Trish Blackwell

My eyes tear up a little as Ellie twirls herself whimsically on the hardwood floors, perpetually two days overdue for mopping. In my mom-life world, mopping is my nemesis and a battle I often lose to the yogurt on the floor, the toys scattered all over, and the muddy paw prints from the dog that undo my efforts as immediately as they are done.

From the perch of my kitchen table I watch the spectacle of our morning routine unfold. It involves dancing, tickling the sleeping dog to wake him, unveiling every toy from the princess castle that had been neatly put away, and—being a generally curious and inquisitive two-year-old—getting into everything. Sometimes the activities vary. Sometimes she pours her orange juice into the dog's water bowl, and sometimes she hides her breakfast fruit in various nooks and crannies throughout the house to find later, but one thing holds true: she always plays with her belly button.

Ellie Belly. I didn't want that to be her nickname. We chose Ellie's name in honor of my grandmother—a beautiful, kind, and patient soul—as a namesake legacy. My only hesitation with our choice was the fear that she might be teased as an "Ellie Belly." My fear stemmed from years of living with an eating disorder that had dominated my life. I am now many years in recovery and much more knowledgeable about how casual cruelty can turn a beautiful name into a reason for Ellie to hate her name and her body. I didn't want her to face the same challenges I had.

Never, in all of the hours (read: day, weeks, and spreadsheets) I spent laboring over baby name lists did I anticipate calling her Ellie Belly myself. The nickname started before she even turned one, and not only does it uniquely suit her, but most surprising of all is that it has a deep meaning that melts my heart. Ellie Belly carries more beauty to it than my maternal heart could have been prepared to understand.

Ellie's belly routine started so young that I cannot remember her without it. Right thumb in the mouth. Left hand plucking or stroking the belly button, over and over. And over and over. Hours on end. In Ellie's world, there is no thumb sucking without belly-button touching. By the time she was nine months old, this self-soothing process turned the hallowed area where the umbilical cord had detached around and inside out, turning her innie into an outie. Her pediatrician confirmed that she had indeed undone whatever stitches were sutured in place at her birth and commended Ellie on her commitment to self-soothing.

Months passed and our days were filled with highs and lows, and through it all belly-button soothing. In the world of parenting where unpredictability is rampant and a child's interests are fleeting, my daughter's love for her belly button turned out to be constant. And, because of this, over time I fell in love with the beauty of this tiny body part we all carry with us and too often overlook. More than a birth scar, this little belly button is a memento of my connection to her. It is our special bond. It kept us intimately connected for over forty weeks before we even met each other face-to-face. It was the physical connection that linked my heartbeat to hers.

She may not realize it, but her belly-button attachment fills those deep wells of my mom heart with purpose. I delight in seeing her love the one thing that made us inseparable. I think about my own belly button and the blood and life it represents from my own mother, and I feel a generational connection that is unshakable and powerfully fulfilling. The belly button chases away loneliness and connects us to all of the mothers in our family tree.

There's also the downside to Ellie's belly-button obsession. Clothing her in the morning for car rides, naps, and bedtime are all strategic efforts to make sure she can always reach her favorite little worry stone. Rompers don't work for Ellie. They are too tight in the arms and neck for her to shove an arm toward her belly, and they don't have open buttons on the front for her to lance her finger through to reach that sacred spot. I have to be careful when I buckle her into the car seat: if I haven't arranged a proper access point for her to caress her belly button, the entire drive will be filled with tears and shrieks. She loves dresses, but since she pulls them up to her shoulders and walks around with her legs, belly, and chest showing, we are left mostly with outfits consisting of the basics for easy, and appropriate, access: pants and shirts. I count it a blessing that she has long hair for a two-year-old because I can always style her hair, even when I can't style her clothes.

Unfortunately, making these little decisions for her has a short life span. Every day she grows further away from me; every day getting more and more independent, daring and autonomous. Her individuality and extraversion ignite within me a maternal ache I never knew existed before Ellie. It's the ache of knowing that these moments, short years filled with very long days, are fleeting.

One day soon she will go to school and her classmates might decide that the name Ellie is too short and the nickname "belly" should be its perfect companion. If that day comes when she steps off the bus, reaching for my hugs and kisses and comfort, I will remind her about her belly button. I will tell her how she and I are always connected. I will tell her that even though we won't always be together, I will always be with her. I will whisper to her that even when she outgrows being my reliable sidekick and mini-me, I have joy knowing that part of me, a reminder of our God-given bond, will never be removed. Where she goes, I will go. Always. And that gives us both strength.

Names are not always what they seem.

MARK TWAIN,

Following the Equator: A Journey Around the World

Part 8

Mother Love

Love heals. Heals and liberates. I use the word love, not meaning sentimentality, but a condition so strong that it may be that which holds the stars in their heavenly positions and that which causes the blood to flow orderly in our veins.

MAYA ANGELOU,
Mom & Me & Mom

41

The Deep End of Love

Kari Kampakis

I should have been exhausted, but I wasn't.

I needed to sleep, but I couldn't.

Instead, I only wanted to look at my new baby girl, an eight-pound miracle named Ella. After 18 hours of labor, she arrived around midnight. As we settled into a hospital room, our surroundings dark and quiet, I savored a moment alone with her.

The nurse had left to gather supplies. My husband was getting food. And I...well, I was undergoing a major transformation.

With adoring eyes I studied Ella's face, memorizing features and wishing I could watch her all night, every night. When our eyes met, she held my gaze, never once wavering. It felt like a reunion, not an introduction, two long-lost friends who already knew and understood each other.

If ever I'd questioned my existence, wondered what good I added to this world, I now had an answer.

This angel from heaven was here because of me. God had chosen me to raise her. As a tidal wave of love swelled inside me, so powerful and intense I could hardly breathe, I suddenly realized something: for this tiny creature to evoke so many life-changing emotions, she had to be special.

Then and there, my life split into two: *Before* and *After*.

Before I became a mom, I'd experienced love in many shapes and forms. I'd given it and taken it, doling out more when someone treated me right, less when they hurt me.

But what I felt for Ella was completely one-sided and unmeasured. Gone was any instinct to protect my heart, because my overwhelming urge was a drive to protect *her*. I knew Ella would never love me the way I loved her, but I didn't care. In fact, that was the beauty of this situation.

At 30 years old, I *wanted* to be saved from my selfishness. I *wanted* motherhood to help me grow up and mature. As I cradled Ella in my arms, the concept of unconditional love sank in. In mere moments she'd stolen my heart like no one ever had. I loved her not because of what she'd done, or might do down the road, but because she existed.

That was enough.

Ella will soon turn 15, and for me that marks 15 years of motherhood. Her birth day was the best day of my life, not because I love Ella more than her sisters, but because she's the one who made me a mom. She was the game changer, the one who took me out of floaties and launched me into the deep end of love.

I was nervous and scared, but somehow I knew how to tread water. Somehow I understood the connection between everyone in the deep end, where staying afloat was the common battle.

My life felt out of control...and yet so free. I'd traded in security for a danger zone, a place where my feet would never touch bottom again. Why would I do that? Why would I take on the risk of drowning?

I'll tell you why: because life begins in the deep end. And for me, it took a child to make me jump in. Ella's birth was like a rebirth for me, a second chance to embrace life with more joy and vulnerability. Never again would I be able to completely harness my feelings, for I'd joined the ranks of women who take on the highs and lows of this world on a deeper, more spiritual level.

And while I liked to reminisce about my days in the shallow end, remembering how carefree life used to be, I didn't wish to go back. In the deep end I came ALIVE; I wanted to soak it up.

Maybe life was easier before Ella, but it wasn't full, or anywhere near complete. Going back could never satisfy me as it had before, because once you experience the deep end, shallow waters aren't the same.

And so I thank my beautiful, kind, and quick-witted firstborn for granting me this experience. I thank her for bearing with me as I learn new strokes in every stage of parenting. Most of all, I thank Ella for her compassion toward others. With her in the universe, I have faith in the future, because I know she'll make it better.

I love you, sweet Ella, not because of what you've done or might do down the road with your many talents, *but because you exist.* It was enough at your birth, and it's enough now. To watch you blossom on this intricate level, as your proud and ever-amazed mother, is a gift for which I am so very, very grateful.

A comfort zone is a beautiful place
but nothing ever grows there.

AUTHOR UNKNOWN

42

In Sickness and in Health

Jennifer Dukes Lee

I lay in a feverish curl, dressed in footie pajamas, while Mom watched the mercury rise in a thin, glass tube.

With one hand, she held a thermometer under my tongue, and with the other, she stroked a terry cloth, damp and cool, across my throbbing brow.

Today as I am writing this, nine days from Mother's Day, this is the place where my memory of mother-love burns strongest: right in the middle of my childhood sick days at home.

It was nothing serious, just the flu or a cold. But mother-love felt like this: arms cradling a bent body. Love smelled like Vicks VapoRub and calamine lotion and liquid amoxicillin. Love sparkled fizzy, like 7-Up in a tall Daffy Duck glass, sweating onto a metal TV tray. Mother-love looked like the tiny Snoopy figurine that she set down by the cartoon glass while I was sleeping.

Mother-love sounded like feet padding double-time on creaky oak-planked floors to help a whimpering child reach the bucket in time.

That's why I never minded being sick as a kid. Because it meant that love was about to come dancing into the room, popping its head through the doorway and wearing a crazy Halloween mask or singing a silly song in exaggerated vibrato.

It's not that Mom didn't love me on the days when I bounded through the house healthy and happy. But the sick days? Those were the best because she stroked my cheeks and tucked stray strands of hair behind my ears.

Mom would wrap me in an afghan cocoon on the couch—she called it a davenport—and turn on the Zenith color console. I watched through half-open eyelids as Big Bird tried to convince his friends that Mr. Snuffleupagus was real.

And Mom would love the sick right out of me.

By the time I traded in Muppets for Maybelline, our relationship skidded a bit. I don't know how it happened, really, but we started to argue. I became Queen of the Eye Roll. Which paired nicely with my favorite word: *Whatever.*

Sure, I still loved Mom, but I didn't act like it. I deserved a big, fat time-out, that's what. The things that seemed to charm everyone else—her silly pranks and her tendency to be the very last person out of church—were the things that annoyed me most. She once chased my friends through the house while wielding a cow tongue. They, of course, found her hilarious. I think I did too, though I hid my laugh behind my eye roll.

I was eager to leave home for college, away from rules.

But even college girls catch colds. I remember dialing her from the dorm, wishing she would bring me 7-Up with ice clinking against a cartoon glass.

Now I'm all grown up. I'm the mom, and I'm pretty sure that time is turning over on itself. I stroke sweaty foreheads and deliver carbonated drinks with straws and silly songs. I am also the last one out of church, and I have begun to publicly embarrass my children whenever those delicious opportunities present themselves.

One spring Mom fell ill. She lost weight and energy and, sadly, some of her zippy humor. We waited and waited for a diagnosis.

A few days before Mother's Day, Dad called. "Pray hard," he said. "Mom's getting sicker by the day."

Our youngest daughter, Anna, came in the room and saw me crying as I stuffed clothes in a duffel bag.

"I know why you're going to see Mema," she said. "It's because when you were little, she always helped you when you were sick. And now you want to help her when she's sick. Right, Mommy?"

Anna was right. I had to go home. *I just had to.* There was a long overdue favor to repay and a sick mama who needed to hear a silly love song.

—

Mom was sick for many months with a mysterious illness that was never fully diagnosed. But later that year she was healed physically. Today Mom is doing great, and believe me, she is as rambunctious as ever. I love you, Mom. Happy Mother's Day. Thanks for taking such good care of me, and teaching me what it means to be a mom, and how to love the least of these, and show grace to my neighbor...and also to myself.

Mother is a verb. It's something you do. Not just who you are.

CHERYL LACEY DONOVAN,
The Ministry of Motherhood

43

To My Water Baby on Your Birthday

Alia Joy

You were my only water baby.

All we had known was how your brother screeched when we lowered him into the tub as a slippery infant, but you sank in right away and let the water cover your shoulders. From the first bath at the hospital to the tiny, blue plastic tub we set up on the kitchen sink, you were always our little fish.

You didn't cry when the water from the little plastic cup would spill across your forehead or trickle into your eyes. You'd grab giant fistfuls of water and try to bring them to your mouth, frustrated that the water spilled through your chubby fingers before you could get it into your mouth. You'd pound balled-up fists into the bubbles and squeal when they'd catch the wind and float around you.

Your little legs would pump with delight when you saw the water being drawn, and I knew you were your father's daughter.

I met him where waves rush, and we breathed salted air and open skies. I see all the things I love about him in you. And now when we visit the ocean, or lakes so cold they make others wince in pain, I know you're going to plunge right in.

You've always been this way. Our little fish. Our water lover, coming out with fingertips wrinkled and aged, like you'd spent a lifetime in the waves.

And I remember how different you felt when you floated in my belly. You swished just like a fish. All smooth movements, limbs gliding along my insides. Your brothers were all fists and knees and solid jabs that left me wondering if they would be drummers, or boxers, or if my insides were going to make it through the pregnancy with the beatings they were getting. But you were like a little fish right from the beginning. Gentle and fluid, like an embrace. And you've always been that gift to us. Gentleness. Adventure. Joy. Grace.

You bring a gentleness to my mothering. I was sharper before you.

I am sea glass now, sharp edges worn smooth by the lapping of your soul into my life day after day, translucent and beautiful. I count myself blessed when you tell me so.

You see your mama in ways I never could have imagined as a girl. When you say you want to be like me when you grow up, I realize mothering redeemed so many of my broken parts. You light up when you see me in red lipstick, tell me how fancy I look, pick out my earrings, or sit cuddled next to me when I read aloud, and you're transfixed by story too.

You ask me to tell you yours over and over. You love hearing about your birth or the time you dressed up for Halloween as a flower fairy with sparkly hair and glittery makeup only to don a Halo battle helmet and carry around a weapon at the last minute. Doesn't this say it all? Glimmering fairy wings and blue eyeshadow under a thick, black plastic visor toting a semiautomatic taser gun. When your tiny four-year-old voice said, "Trick or treat," I wonder what they made of you. I beamed because you never once thought to care.

You are your own person, your own brave soul. Your story is beautiful. You leap into life with your whole heart. You make me live fuller.

You made me a mama to a girl, and I have never recovered from the blessing. I don't imagine I ever will. From the first strokes of glittery polish on fingernails as tiny as baby petals to the times you've skinned knees and made forts and showed up to battle bad guys in your ninja costume or princess gown, you've stolen my heart. You are both fierce and gentle, something I've learned from watching how you care for those around you. I've never seen those two qualities done so well in one little person. The mix of flash and will and grace and gentleness.

So it's fitting that we call you our water baby now. Our little fish, tossing yourself into the water, hair soaked and glinting like scales. You always had that way about you. You are my only water baby.

To my most favorite girl in the whole world on your ninth birthday. A story of you. You are loved with an almost absurd measure. I couldn't fathom how my heart would stretch wide in mothering you, but I know it grows each year. I love the girl you've been and the woman you're becoming.

With all my heart,
Your mama

Being a mother means that your heart is no longer yours; it wanders wherever your children do.

ANONYMOUS

44

Holding My Daughter's Hand

Wynter Pitts

With one simple grasp, her entire world was wrapped into the palm of my hand.

Speechless. Breathless. But like we all do, I counted—

one two three four five

And then again.

six seven eight nine ten

They were all there. Ten of the smallest fingers I had ever seen.

On this day, day one, I held on tight and without saying a word I was immediately and eternally connected to her—my first of four daughters.

Her hand. My hand. Our journey began.

For months we held hands while she ate, while she slept, and while she silently absorbed the new world surrounding her.

At one year old, we held hands as she wobbled across the playground, trying to find her own strength.

At three years old, as she became too independent to be strapped down, we held hands as we strolled aisles and sidewalks together, searching for things we needed and a few things we just liked.

At six years old, we held hands as she, full of excitement and uncertainty, boldly entered a room full of unfamiliar faces and took her place at the seat marked "Alena."

And today, at this tender, awkward, and vulnerable age of 13, we still hold hands. Embarking upon the twists and turns of teen years, we hold hands while we talk, while we read, while we pray, and sometimes while we just sit quietly, snuggled on a couch in an empty room.

Holding my daughter's hand has and continues to be a potent form of understanding between us. It has become our silent language and a secret weapon that takes me right to the most tender places of her heart.

So I am committed to holding on.

Not solely because she doesn't have words to express herself. Not because she's not strong enough to stand on the strength of her own ankles. And not because she needs me to comfort her in a room full of strangers.

I hold her hand because I want her to know that no matter how strong she gets, I am still here. Loving, guiding, praying, protecting, and comforting her.

I love a good conversation with each of my daughters. But I have learned that the best conversations begin with silence.

So, when she needs to talk, when she is ready to talk, I am within the reach of her arm, holding her hand just like the day we first met.

Enough, if something from our hands have power
To live, and act, and serve the future hour.

WILLIAM WORDSWORTH,
"Valedictory Sonnet to the River Duddon"

45

Small Expressions

Kim Hyland

It's an odd-size legal pad. Typical yellow, but about five by seven inches, like a photo.

No. 362-L || EFFICIENCY JUNIOR LEGAL PAD || 50 Sheets

I know it's at least 48 years old, because that's how old I am. And like a photo, it has captured precious memories.

The first page has the words "Likes, continued" written across the top left-hand side. I'd recognize the beautiful penmanship anywhere. It's my mom's.

To stack things up (such as boxes)

To say bye-bye when someone is leaving

To feed herself

Take her bath with toys

To shut doors (sometimes she locks herself in a room)

These are still some of my favorite things, especially that last one.

Small, round paper tabs edge the left side of the EFFICIENCY JUNIOR LEGAL PAD. They create categories, and the first reads "Dislikes." This should be interesting.

Getting her hands & face washed after she eats

*Going to bed (Her bedtime is between 7:30–8:30
—earlier if she's fussy)*

Getting dressed & undressed

Having her hair brushed

Getting her nose cleaned

And so on.

Pretty normal stuff. Reflecting on the six children I've raised, I think how similar baby likes and dislikes seem to be. But to my mom, this was all brand-new. It was noteworthy, and she wrote it down in her beautiful penmanship, in red ink, and categorized.

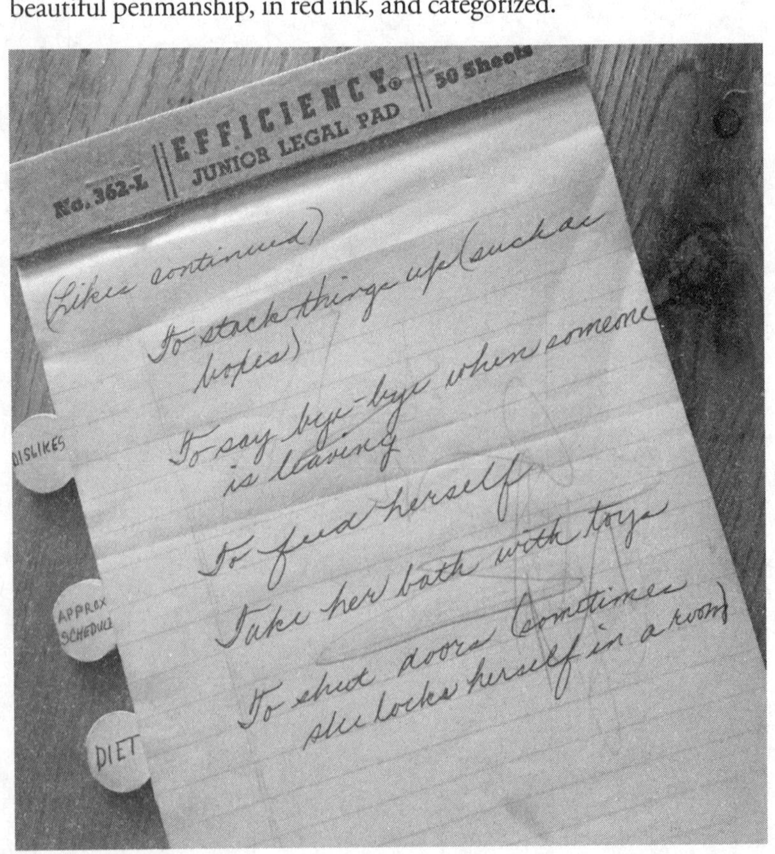

(Likes continued)

To stack things up (such as boxes)

To say bye-bye when someone is leaving

To feed herself

Take her bath with toys

To shut doors (sometimes she locks herself in a room)

Mom was 18 when I was born. Like any young mother, I'm certain she was nervous. I remember my own detailed recordings of wet and poopy diapers, how many times my first had nursed, whether he burped, how long he slept, etc. For some of us, like Mom and me, there's something about putting pen to paper that tames the fear of the unknown.

Her words, written as instructions for a sitter or a relative over the weekend, are careful observations of a mother's love. Only a mother knows her child like this, and now I'm getting to know myself in a new way.

APPROX. SCHEDULE

6:30–7:00 *Usually wakes up and has bottle of warm milk*

8:00–8:30 *Breakfast*

11:30–12:00 *Ready for nap & noon bottle of milk*
(or juice for nap & milk in cup for lunch)

1:30–2:00 *Lunch when she wakes*

She continues, outlining my evening schedule, including an asterisked note clarifying how many times I should be bathed weekly.

I can't help but smile at the details. These are the kinds of things a mom typically fusses over only once. A second child comes along and she's happy just to feed them two to three good meals and get in one good nap.

Mom liked to write things down. When she passed away three years ago, my dad found a multitude of papers and pages recording her thoughts, prayers, scriptures, and family memories. She even had a journal of my kids' firsts, funny things they said, and cute habits.

Her last few years she'd taken to writing a gratitude journal. She filled four, and her numbered prayers of thanksgiving were well into the thousands. Words can't describe the comfort it brought our family as we read her heart on those pages.

The instructions for my care continue:

DIET

Favorite food–American cheese

She is supposed to be able to eat anything you eat—but she won't eat except what she likes.

Followed by detailed suggestions and combinations for each meal.

A mother's love is a living thing. Even its smallest expressions continue to warm, soothe, and encourage long after they're first conveyed. My mom had no idea that almost half a century after she wrote these words, I would read them and still feel her love, tender care, and attention.

SLEEPING HABITS

Bedtime: *7:30–8:30 p.m.*

Attire: *PJs*

Overnight Pamper

Bottle of warm milk

Thank you, Mom. Good night. I'll see you in the morning.

I remember my mother's prayers and they have always followed me. They have clung to me all my life.

ABRAHAM LINCOLN

46

Motherhood and Cleanup on Aisle Four

Katie Kenny Phillips

It took me a while before I could walk past the dairy section of the grocery store without having flashbacks. In my memory, the song always came on right when I hit the yogurt, always the same song, as if proving the effective use of piped-in music or the predictability of my shopping habits or maybe both. It bore through the layers of my heart like a scalpel, but truthfully, I probably would have found symbolism in an elementary school band's wild rendition of "Hot Cross Buns." I carried a lot of thoughts around in my head and heart those days.

There it was, that song, playing as if for my ears only, and I would look at my darling baby and cry. Right there in front of the yogurt. I'd put on my sunglasses, and it always helped to stick my nose in that sweet baby neck because nuzzles can hide tears and dispense genuine love all at the same time. Oh, this foster care journey. No one told me. No one could have prepared me for it.

When I heard that song, I looked around at the people in the store and thought incredulously, *Do you hear this? Can you feel the pain radiating off me like the sun? When this baby goes home, I will feel like my daughter has* died*!* I would see mothers walking around with little girls a few years older than mine and they took my breath away. I felt like I was leaving a trail behind me in that neighborhood store—small, shattered heart crumbs, revealing where I had come from so I'd hopefully be able to find my way home.

That's heavy for the dairy aisle.

But I wondered sincerely how I was supposed to find my way home while on this adventure of foster care. You get training, but not for this.

There *is* no training on sacred suffering.

As soon as you say yes, you forfeit your right to ever see life the same way again. You cannot unsee the trauma and the stories and real-life wounds. You cannot unfeel the bone-marrow-deep love you have for a child. And you cannot escape the real and true uncertainty of what will ever become of them. Or you, for that matter. Everything changes.

But I wouldn't go back even if I could.

This particular child of mine, content with waving a fat, little wrist at fellow shoppers, was my daughter from the very beginning. I held her for the first time at four months old. I kissed her belly and watched her breathe in her sleep. She was my daughter in every sense except for legally, of course. It was a strange place to stand, one foot on either side of a dividing line. One heart split, as if it couldn't reside in the same chest. I couldn't reconcile why she felt like my forever child, yet on paper, according to the court, this child was destined to go home. And I couldn't reconcile wanting to keep this child while at the same time loving the birth mother and wanting her to succeed. What to do, what to think? What to pray?

Foster care is not for wimps.

So there I stood, hearing the words of the song, and considering the fact that if my daughter went home, I may never be able to shop in this store again. With the music and the dairy aisle and the memories—a potential catastrophic mess fallen from the shelves in an earthquake of my own pain. What would our life look like a year from then? Or ten? Would I always look at other people's daughters in the grocery store and think of my own? Would I wonder if her wrists were still adorably fat or if she still waved at strangers?

If I saw her would she wave at me?

Mother Teresa once said, "Yesterday is gone. Tomorrow has not yet come. We have only today. Let us begin."

So I did as all of us mothers do. Every day. I began and began and began again. I shopped for groceries, walked the aisles, and kissed the neck with uncertainty and fear and great, great love.

And I *have* returned to that store, for inquiring minds. Many times, in fact. With the darling baby now turned beautiful young girl. I still hear music; they still play songs on a loop. And the crumbs I dropped? I faithfully kept dropping them, day after day, year after year, and I did eventually find my way home. With her. Everything has changed—nearly four years has a way of doing that—and she is now, in every single possible sense of the word, my daughter. My *daughter*. The court has told me so.

That *is* heavy for the dairy aisle. And music to my ears.

In all the world, there is no heart for me like yours.
In all the world, there is no love for you like mine.

MAYA ANGELOU

Part 9

Leaving a Legacy

The mercy of the LORD is from everlasting to everlasting upon them that fear him, and his righteousness unto children's children.

PSALM 103:17

47

Not the Dream I Thought It Would Be

Deidra Riggs

Drop me off at a paint store and you won't have to come looking for me for hours. Send me a year's supply of HGTV or *Better Homes and Gardens* magazines and you are guaranteed a solid week of silence as far as I'm concerned. Not a peep.

I get it honestly, yet unintentionally, from my mother.

My mother never sat me down and said, "This is what it takes to make a house feel cozy and safe. This is what you need to buy and this is the color you need to paint if you want a house that spreads its arms wide to welcome you home." My mother is a violinist, not an interior designer. And yet I've always thought the editors of those home-decorating magazines would swoon over the rooms in my mother's house.

Of course, I may be biased.

She never said it, but I'm pretty sure my mom was hoping I'd follow in her footsteps and choose the violin. I still have the tiny instrument my parents purchased for me when I was in elementary school. It's in a case, somewhere in the basement of my house. I can't tell you the last time it was touched.

Here's what I remember about playing the violin: it hurt my fingers and my collarbone, and it gave me a cramp in my neck. Not my cup of tea. Not by a long shot. Sorry, Mom.

When it became clear the violin and I were considerably less than a match made in heaven, I remember I switched to the flute. My mom said she'd played the flute in college. Or was it the piccolo? Either way, the thing I remember most about the flute was the dizzy feeling I always had after blowing across the mouthpiece in my orchestra class at school. I liked the flute better than the violin, but not enough to stick with it.

And so there were piano lessons. Years and years of piano lessons, with my mother sitting beside me on the piano bench to make sure I practiced and that my fingers on the keyboard kept up with the ticking of the metronome. I learned to read music, I pressed through some boring recitals, I played for my parents' dinner guests (the horror!), and once I even accompanied (oh so reluctantly) the congregational hymn before my husband's sermon (the memory of *that* piano-playing fiasco makes me shudder to this day).

I think we all sort of hope we're passing on something meaningful to our children. I believe we dream we might leave them something of substance that will tell the world we were here, we were loved, and we left behind something that mattered to us. I think we sometimes want our children to love what we love, just because we love it so much. And sometimes I think we want our children to live out the dreams we never realized for ourselves.

I only say these things because I'm a mom myself now. My children are grown and gone. They're doing things I never dreamed possible, but that's mainly because there was no way I could have dreamed up the things it is now possible to do in this world. But I'd be lying if I said I didn't have dreams for them when they were born.

For a very long time I tried to shape my children into a form I had carved out for them. I folded over their edges and squeezed their thoughts, and I tried to shave down their options to just the ones I thought were acceptable, or meaningful, or (dare I say it?) holy.

Thank God (and I mean that) they didn't cave to my wishes.

One afternoon, when my son had graduated from college and was visiting for the Thanksgiving holiday, he looked at me and said, "It must be hard, Mom."

I was busy basting the turkey or buttering the rolls, and I wasn't quite sure what he meant. So I said, "Why do you say that?"

"Well," my son answered, "I imagine when you have a baby, you look at that baby in your arms and dream all sorts of things for their life."

"Yes," I said, resting one hand on my hip as I leaned against the refrigerator.

"So it must be hard," my son continued, "when that child grows up and follows a different dream."

It is hard. Or at least it was. It was hard until I stopped holding so tightly to the dreams I had for my children and let them go.

Don't rush past that, though. Don't get me wrong. Letting them go was terribly difficult! I don't know if I've ever done anything more difficult than that. It was like prying my fingers off a long-lost treasure and releasing it into some dimension just beyond my reach or my ability to control.

But isn't that the point? Our children are born to live their own abundant lives. They are given gifts and talents and experiences and passions and interests and relationships and skills and desires that are uniquely designed to take them into the world and chart their own course. As much as we want to, we can't chart that course for them. As hard as it may be to watch them follow their own dreams, there comes a point where we have to let them go.

Thank God (and I mean that) my mom didn't force those music lessons on me. Eventually she let me go, and I landed on my own two feet with a love of color and textures and cozy beds and screened-in porches. Just like my mom.

In between all those music lessons, my mom was also taking me to the wallpaper store and the paint store. She let me choose my own colors for my bedroom. She let me pick out my own curtains and bedspreads. She let me write my name on the living room walls before my dad covered it over with fern-printed wallpaper.

When overnight guests came to visit, my mom never told me I

couldn't pretend we were running a bed-and-breakfast. She let me print menus for our guests, and she told me I'd done a wonderful job of making up the beds with fresh sheets and stocking the bathroom with clean towels.

I don't think she knew the impact she was making on me.

I inherited a love of design and hospitality from my mom. It was her unintended gift. While she and I sat on that piano bench together, my bare feet rested on the white shag carpet that was all the rage and my stomach rumbled at the delicious fragrances coming from the kitchen. When she set the table for a dinner party, I took notes. When she showed me lamplight makes a home feel so much cozier than overhead flush-mounted ceiling lights, I never forgot it. When she insisted on a house with a fireplace that worked, it didn't take long for me to understand why. When my mom lit candles at the dinner table each night, no matter who was there or what we were eating, her attention to detail left an indelible mark on my heart.

To this day, walking through the door of my parents' home fills me with warmth and a feeling of safety and an abundance of love. It is the most beautiful legacy my mother could possibly have given to me. On a crisp autumn night, when I set the table for dinner and light the candles and turn up *Adagio for Strings* on my iPhone, I am living the legacy my mother passed on to me. And when my daughter texts me and says, "Want to go with me to HomeGoods?" my quick response is always, "Yes!"

Small cheer and great welcome
makes a merry feast.

WILLIAM SHAKESPEARE,
The Comedy of Errors

48

The Sisters at the Beach

Kendra Burton

Although I already knew Jesus's saving grace and had been baptized, I really learned how to live with Him when we began spending a week each summer at the beach with my grandmother and her sisters. These women raised my mother, but here at the ocean The Sisters turned their attention to me.

Each morning one of my great-aunts would quietly open my bedroom door and whisper, "Kenny!" softly enough not to wake anyone else in the room, and then I would slip out and meet them on the porch. Alyne always had a coffee waiting for me—really she had milk, sugar, and a splash of coffee waiting for me—and if my mom was still asleep, Nancy would sneak me a dessert. There's nothing like pound cake or cream cheese bars first thing in the morning! The sisters would sit in a line of rocking chairs in their robes, coffee in hand, and I would sit in front of one of them, usually my beloved Tommye, and just listen.

Then they worshipped. But not in a traditional, just singing songs kind of way. Really worshipped. They reminisced and told me their stories. They recounted mistakes they made and recalled God's grace. They remembered joy and were thankful for it. They told me about their hardworking parents who loved them; their live-in maid whom they adored; their grandparents; roller skating up hills by holding on to the fender of a moving car; unhappy marriages, happy marriages, and widowhood; what it's like to lose a child to an illness that could easily be prevented now: both the joys and the heartaches of life. Interspersed among the stories were the hymns: "In the Garden," "The Old Rugged Cross," "How Great Thou Art." One started singing, and before the third word, they all joined in. And oh, how they could sing! From Grammy's soprano to Alyne's husky tenor—their voices were beautiful to me.

They talked about Jesus and to Jesus as if He were sitting on the porch with us. As if they could touch Him or hear His response. This particularly fascinated my young-girl self. I never knew about Jesus in the *midst* of life. I thought He was at church, loving me from church, waiting to be worshipped and learned about at church—see the church theme? But for them, Jesus was practical.

It's the most valuable lesson they taught me: Jesus *is* practical. Jesus is with us in the good, the bad, and the ugly. At that young age I only thought He was in the good; the bad and the ugly happened when He wasn't around. The Sisters not only showed me something new, but over the course of twelve summers they cemented it in me.

When your child dies of appendicitis at age nine, it's not that Jesus wasn't around; He is the answer to that pain. When your husband passes away suddenly, leaving you with three teenage daughters, it's not that Jesus wasn't there; He is the answer to that grief. When your marriage is hard, it's not that Jesus isn't around; He is the answer to the hard. It is this practicality they taught me.

It's been many years since those summer days at the beach; only Grammy and Great-Aunt Billie remain. But I sometimes wonder if other people were nourished by the early-morning worship of the Willard Sisters. Did snatches of hymns carry on ocean breezes to other porches? Do other people in this world sometimes miss those lovely voices? The lessons learned on those lazy summer mornings sustain me to this day.

Where two or three are gathered together in my name, there am I in the midst of them.

MATTHEW 18:20

49

An Island Legacy

Kelli Stuart

We ambled up the path that morning, sweat already trickling down our backs as the sun beat down from its perch in the Caribbean sky. Seagulls cawed overhead, their raucous cheer leading the way like a welcome parade. I gazed to my left and took in the sight of the crystal-blue water that lapped at the rocky shore nearby.

"Here it is," she said softly.

I looked up and shaded my eyes, taking in the sight of the house I knew so well from photographs but had never before seen in real life. It was crumbling and faded, a weary replica of the structure I'd studied in those pictures. A large tree lay against it, evidence of a hurricane that had blown through the spring before.

"Should we look inside?" I asked.

My mom took a tentative step forward and peered into the gaping hole where there once stood a door.

"We can try," she said. Carefully we stepped across the gravelly, sandy threshold toward the rickety front porch. We froze when a low growl pierced through the salty air. A mangy dog had appeared in the open doorway, and he made it perfectly clear we were to step no farther.

"It's the ghost of Mr. Stubbs," my mom whispered. She said it with a smile on her face, but she was only half joking. Very slowly we made our retreat, stepping back across the threshold and onto the sandy street. I watched my mom as she gazed at the building that housed her childhood memories.

We were in South Caicos where my mom spent the formative years of her youth as a missionary kid. My grandparents were pioneer missionaries to the Turks and Caicos Islands in the early '60s. When I mention this, I'm often met with starry-eyed stares and exclamations of "Wow! What a place to grow up. They really suffered for Jesus, didn't they?"

But in fact, they *did* suffer, for these were the days before Turks and Caicos was a desired resort destination.

They lived without electricity or running water. They were at the mercy of the ocean that surrounded their perimeter, and sometimes waited far too long for supply ships to arrive with necessary items. To this day my mom can't even look at a can of Spam without gagging.

It wasn't easy growing up on that tiny island. They were often sick, and because there was no school for my mom and her older brother, they had to leave their family and fly back to the States each fall to attend boarding school, often hitching rides with strangers on small airplanes in order to make their way back to Miami in time for the first day.

There's nothing about that time that is glamorous when my mom talks about it, but her voice is *always* laced with nostalgia. There was a simplicity to her youth that one doesn't come by anymore. Her days were spent wandering the island with her friends, fishing off the coast, and always avoiding the ghost of Mr. Stubbs, which islanders swore lived inside her house.

Mom and I wound our way back up the street, her stealing glances back at her childhood home and me stealing glances at her. It was interesting watching her process this trip. She is tough as nails, my mom, not one for complaining or verbally processing her emotions. But that day I could see her sifting quietly through the memories.

We rounded the corner, her old house disappearing from sight, and saw two older women sitting in rocking chairs on their front porch. My mom smiled and waved, and they returned the gesture.

"Good morning," she said, her Bahamian accent seeping out in her words. It had reappeared the second we landed in the islands.

"I'm Candy," she offered. "I'm Jim Cooper's daughter. Did you know him?"

One of the women leaned forward, her eyes growing wide. "You Jim Cooper's daughter?" she exclaimed. My mom nodded her head. The woman threw her head back with a grin and clapped her hands.

"Oh, I loved your daddy!" she cried. "And your mama was one of a kind! I knew your parents, yes. Der ain't neva been anyone quite like Pastah Jim and Aunt Betty."

My mom blinked back tears, and so did I. This wasn't the first conversation like this we'd had. Two days earlier we had walked the back streets of North Caicos where my grandfather founded a little church, and we came across an old man working in his front yard. When my mom showed him an old black-and-white picture she'd found in her mother's photo album, his eyes filled with tears.

"Das me right dere," he said, pointing. "And das my brutha. He's already with de Lord. I loved your mama and your daddy. Dese islands is not da same, tanks to your parents. Your daddy brought the news of Jesus to dese islands."

We returned back to our hotel late that afternoon after a day spent talking to local residents and walking down literal memory lanes. It was hot and dry, so we walked to the pool, which overlooked the crystal-blue ocean, and we lowered ourselves into the lukewarm water.

I watched as my mom drank it all in, the landscape so seared into her heart that it almost felt like a holy moment. She had shared her most precious memories with me, and the impact of that wasn't lost on either of us. I swam up next to her and put my arms up on the edge of the pool. I watched as the sun began its slow descent beneath the horizon and listened as the waves crashed over the rocks below us. It sounded like applause, like hearty praise from the islands that were a part of her, and had now become a part of me too.

I recognized that time as a gift, the pride of family having been handed to me by my mom, wrapped in salty blue water and shimmering in the golden glow of the setting sun. That was my legacy, a rich heritage to be treasured and shared now with my children.

I hold that a strongly marked personality can influence descendants for generations.

BEATRIX POTTER

50

The Blessing of Blackberry Bushes

Kayla Aimee

I grew up spending the dog days of summer in rural Tennessee farmland. The little yellow house that my great-grandparents lived in sat straight across from the cotton fields and just down the gravel road from the lake. The town they lived in was so small that it was home to just one of everything: one grocery store, one gas station, and one single traffic light.

(Well, except for the churches. There are three of those on account of how the town is also smack-dab in the middle of the Bible Belt.)

Large swaths of those summers were spent sitting on the sunporch snapping green beans for dinner, picked fresh from the backyard garden as the day settled into evening. It was my job as a little girl and now it is my little girl's job; she sits at the table, and the crack of each snap ties us together through tradition. Whenever I reflect on my own childhood, I find it is the simplest of moments that have stuck to me. How we would carry tin buckets to the patch of blackberry bushes, staining our fingers as we plucked the ripe berries for Mawmaw to make into cobbler. The way we all chased down the ice cream truck, waving a dollar. These are among my sweetest memories, literally and figuratively.

In an effort to recreate a bit of the country life I was so fond of, we joined a local farm co-op that we visit each week to stock up on fresh groceries. When they opened the blackberry fields up for picking, I knew I wanted to take my three-year-old daughter, Scarlette, with a little tin bucket of her own. She ran through the vines, bubbling over with excitement about learning which berries to choose and "doing it awl by myselfs."

At the end of the morning we measured out our haul on the vintage farm scale and the weight read two and a half pounds. I looked at Scarlette, with her purple-stained mouth and proudly holding her empty bucket, and I thought, *This bunch of blackberries weighs one pound more than what she weighed when she was born.*

Three years earlier it was her on a scale, fresh into the world 15 weeks too early, and the scale they laid her on before swooping her away to the intensive care flashed "one pound, eight ounces." Three years earlier she hung between here and heaven and I never saw this day coming, the one where she would run wide open through a field swinging a bucket.

And in a moment drenched in sun and grace I stood on that farm and I breathed a quick prayer of thanks for blackberries, a healthy child, and the opportunity to pass down a legacy. These are the times that I revel in motherhood, because of unexpected blessings found in blackberry bushes.

And then we made jam.

Train up a child in the way he should go: and when he is old, he will not depart from it.

PROVERBS 22:6

51

Holland Calling

Rachel McMillan

A call from my Oma's family in faraway Holland patched through to the farm town of Clinton, Ontario, made the newspaper more than half a century ago. An emblem of two countries unusually grafted by a world war. My Oma was a war bride, a widow with a young daughter who married a stretcher-bearer with the Canadian Forces and uprooted her life to follow him to the safe haven of Canada.

In our age of social media and immediate connectivity, it is hard to imagine the anticipation through crackling calm before an overseas call. Though my Oma made connections with other immigrants from the Netherlands who, like her, had settled in small Canadian farm towns, it was never the same. There was the home she left behind and the home she forged, scratching the surface of the English language, the memories of Nazi-occupied Holland nipping at her heels.

And while my Oma created her new home, she still sang of how she would "give all of her tomorrows for just one of yesterday." Money was tight, and Oma only went back to Holland for funerals, though the budget hadn't stretched far enough for her own mother's and father's.

I try to imagine Holland calling. A sound from home. How empty and scary it would feel to make a new life while your family lived so far away.

I picture Oma waiting, butterflies in her stomach after a night most likely sleepless with anticipation, the music of the past welling in her like one of the many songs she sang in her broken English. Like Vera Lynn—"We'll meet again"—or the hymns that helped her memorize her new language. Counting the days and the minutes, minutes ticking into eternities in the hours before the call was to come through. Then, from the other side of the Atlantic, the link binding her to all that she had left behind. One infinitesimal moment to speak freely and not check everything through the filter of her brain. Her voice no longer a stream fumbling over the boulder of translation.

Holland called and my Oma's little corner of momentary heaven made a Canadian paper.

As a kid it was a joke. My aunts and my mom making fun of Oma's excitement. "Holland calling" was something my Opa said every time the Dutch relatives would call, the long distance becoming easier as the time passed, no longer headline worthy. Later, he said it every time the phone rang, remembering his deceased wife mistily.

In my childhood, after Oma was gone, Dutch settled in here and there in italicized inflection or an anecdote, in Mom's parts of Oma sticking to me like Velcro. *Oliebolen. Knijper.* And Mom's unpronounceable middle name, *Tjetske.*

I never know when a story will be woven into the tapestry of one of our days. Mom still uses Oma's recipes, carries the torch of Christmas dinner, and purchases blue delft. She recites a cute anecdote from a recent visit to her granddaughters, my nieces, and she gets a glazed look. "Rachel, that is how Oma used to talk about you when you were little." As I understand Oma through my mother, so my mother tried to understand Oma through the power of story, the tales of the life she bravely left behind.

I sit and think of this patchwork quilt of stories and wonder if the image of Oma dims behind my mother's eyes. There is a gentle crack in her resolve to make Christmas light and happy, to host and cook with her mother's recipes, to ensure hot gravy is kept on the table and the pie crusts are rolled by hand. She still tears when "Silent Night" is played. "Oma used to sing that."

I piece together an Oma of hearsay matched with my imagination. Windmill cookies and *klompen* and this horrible licorice candy. Tupperware is durable; you can rinse out plastic sour cream containers for leftovers, keep elastics, and reuse washed tinfoil: a million and one helpful hints from Oma, who lived through a war when nothing went to waste, in an occupied country where people ate tulip bulbs to stave off hunger.

Mom loops more beads onto the string of remembrance, and we collect the normal treasures people take for granted when the person they lost is still daily found.

I call my mom often, me in Toronto, her in a small town two hours north. It isn't newspaper worthy. She listens with her infinite patience about the little parts of my day oh-so-important to me while her stories stay on the shelf. Her opinion framing my portraits of insignificance into something worthy of display. When she was my age, Oma was already in heaven. Now my mother mutes the Stanley Cup playoffs (a very difficult thing for her to do) to wade in my world a while and be my mom.

I imagine Oma still here, pouring coffee, arranging the table, setting out the cream and muffins and cutlery as my mom says she used to do when she would visit her old home on the way to her first teaching position as a young adult. Some mornings I suspect they snapped at each other in stressful sleeplessness; others they spent excavating the humdrum of ordinary days that now seem precious.

Now retired, Mom went back to Amsterdam for a visit. Her eyes glisten with gratitude as she relayed how they all got together—cousins and relatives—and had a big dinner in honor of the Canadian visitors. And her cousins cried when they saw her: a link in their chain to the past.

A cousin from Amsterdam visited Canada a few months later and family barbecues and brunches with children and bustle kept Mom from what she truly wished. "I wish Anita and I had time alone just to talk about Oma."

Holland doesn't call anymore, but it echoes. Echoes through my mom, echoes through my brother and my sister and me, who all have the spirit of nomadic traveling wanderers, revering our country's history, proud of the liberation of a sieged country that brought Oma here. Echoes in the Christmas traditions, the careful unwrapping of ornaments and the stories that accompany them; echoes in a random word in perfect Dutch inflection, in the middle name of my niece, Maisie Susanna.

I realize that my understanding of Oma by way of my mom will be lost somewhat in translation, not unlike the static of a patched intercontinental phone call that crackled over the Atlantic. I'll never quite understand. I only have echoes and anecdotes. It makes me sad sometimes that there is a slice of Mom that I take for granted as she listens and prays for me and supports me and makes me laugh and sends me home from a weekend trip with homemade meals and groceries (even though I am well into my thirties) and fixes a rip on a seam. Now my mom is Oma, carrying on the tradition, squeezing my little nieces, binding another link on the chain of our heritage. And I know that they will hear stories and anecdotes and sentences punctuated with the most surprising insertion of a Dutch word, and Holland will call and echo still.

My heritage has been my grounding,
and it has brought me peace.

MAUREEN O'HARA

52

Like Mother, Like Daughter

Dawn Camp

It's been more than 13 years since the spring day when my mother quietly left this world for the next, the year before our youngest daughter was born. Lily is the only one of our children who never knew her, if even for a short time. Mother passed away on my birthday, and it's taken me years to reclaim the day as my own. For her, those two March 16ths, 38 years apart, began in pain and ended in joy: in the birth of her first child and in the presence of her Savior.

Calling your mom *Mother* sounds formal to some people; I don't mean it that way. She preferred Mommy, and I called her that until the point when I must have thought I'd outgrown it. Mother wouldn't have been Mama any more than she would have been Granny (her grandmother name was Gran); it just didn't suit.

Mother was petite, in poor health for much of her life, and physically weak, but her mind was wise and strong. She didn't understand why family members asked her advice in areas that didn't involve her. It was because we respected her counsel. She liked to say, "No one person is important enough to make everyone around them miserable," although we sometimes encountered people who thought they were that one person.

Mother didn't waste much time in the kitchen. Her cooking didn't extend far beyond Bisquick pancakes and boxed brownies, but she mastered her own, personal version of comfort food: little white powdered doughnuts warmed in the toaster oven until they bubbled; Dr Pepper boiled and then flavored with lemon juice; warm brownies drizzled with melted butter. My sister told me that after I left for college, Mother sometimes sat in her recliner and toasted marshmallows with a lighter to make s'mores. I admire such dedication in pursuit of the perfect snack. I came by my sweet tooth honestly.

As an adult, I've gotten tetanus shots because of unexpected encounters with a rusty nail and the bottom of a go-cart (that's a story for another time), but my mother needed them—twice—because of squirrels. She attempted to rescue one from a dog's mouth and also tried to touch one at a petting zoo. She loved animals, even if they didn't always love her.

Last week a lady at church told me my mother would be proud of me and my family. She passed away before I started writing; missing her inspired me to start my blog. She knew seven of my eight children, but was gone before any of the girls entered their teens. I've missed her advice as they've grown. She would appreciate that her new great-grandson (likely the first of many great-grandchildren) is named after retired pitcher Greg Maddux; she sure did love the Braves.

Time and perspective continue to reveal my mother's influence, the ways I'm like her and the ways I'm not. She hated the color orange; we never had a pillow, a splash of paint, or a piece of clothing in that shade. Mother was never healthy, and once had surgery in a hospital wing painted orange. I'm sure it was meant to be cheerful, but a happy color can't overcome a painful association. I didn't own anything orange in the 20 years I lived on my own as an adult while my mother lived; I never considered it. Now I have orange shirts and orange scarves, and a cute little orange owl decorates our house each fall. I love orange! At first it felt like a betrayal when I realized it, but her experience was not my own.

I believe words have power, and my mother knew it too. She hated the word *snot* but thought *stuff* was a good Bible word. (Genesis 45:20 cautions us, "Regard not your stuff.") *Facetious* was one of her favorites.

Winsome is one of mine. Her shelves overflowed with books, just like mine, and I have no doubt she would have read every word I write.

Although Mother didn't question God's good taste or the beauty of His creation, she thought hydrangeas were tacky and found the big, blue flowers offensive. The summer after she passed I planted a bush in my front yard, in her honor. Please don't think I meant it in disrespect; it wasn't until then that I realized I actually liked hydrangeas, much like the color orange.

I don't prefer her soft pastel color palette, and I've never planted the signature red geraniums that filled the window boxes of my childhood home each spring. She never baked a cake or a pie, but I even make my own yogurt. I can't imagine my mother exercising, even if her health permitted it, but I started running a few years ago and pull out my 30 Day Shred videos religiously each spring. She liked coffee; I drink tea. But in spite of our more obvious differences, in fundamentals my mother and I are much the same: stubbornly independent, unwilling to forsake our core values, intellectually curious, fiercely loyal to family.

I sometimes wonder if my kids listen to me, but I know from experience a mother's words burrow deep in the hearts of her children. Whether we embrace or reject them, they're always a part of us, speaking soft or loud in the voice of our conscience. I'm glad my mother raised me to think for myself and hold fast to my convictions, even the unpopular ones, and that occasionally I'm blessed to hear the words: "You remind me of your mother."

My mother's gifts of courage to me were both large and small. The latter are woven so subtly into the fabric of my psyche that I can hardly distinguish where she stops and I begin.

MAYA ANGELOU,
Mom & Me & Mom

Contributor Biographies

Kayla Aimee is a sweet-tea loving Southern girl and mom to two who finds her joy in sharing stories of hope and humor. She writes about a fruitful life at kaylaaimee.com and is the author of the books *Anchored* and *In Bloom.*

Diane Bailey is a freelance writer and founder of The Consilium—a community of wisdom and purpose. She encourages women with humor and biblical principles about stepfamilies, finding purpose after the nest is empty, and leadership. She blogs about her perfectly imperfect life at www.dianewbailey.net.

Trish Blackwell is a confidence coach, fitness expert, podcaster, and writer. She lives in the DC area with her husband, Brandon Synan, and their two littles, Ellie and Baker. Her first book, *Insecurity Detox: A Breakout Plan to Rejuvenate Your Mind, Body and Spirit*, released in 2016 by Howard.

Kendra Burton is living on coffee, love, and God's Word in the Atlanta area. You can find her in her kitchen making pumpkin spice lattes or at www.kendraathome.com writing about home life and homeschooling.

Dawn Camp is an Atlanta-based writer, wife, mother of eight, and editor and photographer of *The Beauty of Grace*, *The Gift of Friendship*, and *The Heart of Marriage*. She lives with a camera in one hand and a glass of sweet tea in the other, blogs about family, faith, and Photoshop at MyHomeSweetHomeOnline.net, and is a regular contributor to incourage.me.

Mary Carver is a writer, speaker, and recovering perfectionist. She lives for good books, spicy queso, and television marathons, but she lives because of God's grace. Mary writes with humor and honesty about giving up on perfect and finding truth in unexpected places on her blog, MaryCarver.com. She also is a regular contributor to incourage.me, MomAdvice.com, and MothersofDaughters.com.

Kaitlin Curtice is a Native American Christian writer, speaker, and worship leader living in Atlanta. She is an author with Paraclete Press and a blogger at www.kaitlincurtice.com, and writes on the intersection of culture and spirituality.

Married to her college sweetheart and mom to three, **Robin Dance** dreams of Neverland and Narnia. She's a ragamuffin princess and as Southern as sugar-shocked tea. She's sometimes lost, sometimes found, and always celebrates redemptive purpose at robindance.me.

Wendy Dunham is a children's author, mother of two adult children, and therapist for children with special needs. Her two middle-grade novels, *My Name Is River* and *Hope Girl*, are through Harvest House. She also wrote *The Tales of Buttercup Grove*, a series of early readers through Harvest House. Visit her website at www.wendydunham.net.

Elizabeth Foss is the mother of nine (four of them girls), and Nona to two more little girls. She loves good books and long walks that inspire her to break into a run. She is the founder of www.takeupandread.org.

Holley Gerth is a bestselling author of books like *You're Already Amazing*, life coach, and speaker. She also cofounded the website incourage.me and blogs at www.holleygerth.com.

Krista Gilbert is a podcaster, speaker, author, and cofounder of the Open Door Sisterhood. She lives in the mountains of Idaho with her husband and four children. You can find her at kristagilbert.com or theopendoor sisterhood.com.

USA Today bestselling author **Tricia Goyer** is the author of over 70 books, including *Walk It Out: The Radical Result of Living God's Word One Step at a Time*. She is the mom of ten, the grandmother of four, and mentors teen moms in Little Rock, Arkansas. She loves to connect with readers at www.TriciaGoyer.com.

Leah Highfill is a writer and piano instructor, wife to a pastor, mom to two medical miracles, and a dual citizen of Canada and the USA. She hosts an extensive, private, online ministry of encouragement for pastors' wives around the world, and writes hope into their hearts at www.embracin grace.com.

Denise J. Hughes is the author of *Deeper Waters* and *Six Stories Every Mom Should Tell.* She blogs at www.DeniseJHughes.com and serves as the editorial coordinator at (in)courage by DaySpring. She lives in Southern California with her husband and three kids.

Kim Hyland is a writer, speaker, and the founder of the Winsome retreat. Her first book, *An Imperfect Woman: Letting Go of the Need to Have It All Together*, released in February 2018 with Baker Books. Connect with Kim at www.winsomeliving.com.

Alia Joy is a storyteller, speaker, and homeschooling mother of three. She shares her story in broken bits and pieces on her blog, Aliajoy.com, and finds community where others' stories intersect. She's also a regular contributor at Grace Table, SheLoves, and (in)courage.

Kari Kampakis is a mother of four girls as well as an author, blogger, and speaker. Her two books for teen and tween girls, *10 Ultimate Truths Girls Should Know* and *Liked: Whose Approval Are You Living For?*, have been used widely across the country for youth group studies. Kari lives in Birmingham, Alabama, with her family and a mischievous dog named Lola.

Alexandra Kuykendall is the author of *Loving My Actual Life* and *Loving My Actual Christmas.* She lives in Denver with her husband, Derek, and their four daughters. Connect with her at AlexandraKuykendall.com.

Jennifer Dukes Lee is a national speaker and author of *The Happiness Dare* and *Love Idol.* She and her husband, Scott, live on the Lee family farm in Iowa, where they are raising corn, soybeans, pigs, and two humans named Lydia and Anna.

September McCarthy is the wife to one amazing builder and a home educating mother to ten beautiful children. She is juggling the stages of motherhood, from adult children to toddlers, and now is a grandma to two more blessings. She is the author of *Why Motherhood Matters* and blogs at septembermccarthy.com.

Rachel McMillan works in educational publishing by day and writes by night. She is the author of the Herringford and Watts series (Harvest House) and the upcoming Van Buren and DeLuca series (Harper Collins).

Rachel lives in Toronto, Ontario, where she loves to fawn over her two little nieces, read voraciously, and travel near and far.

Elizabeth Maxon is wife to Joey and homeschooling mama to Lucy and Oliver. Her company, Back Porch Press, offers books, videos, and podcasts to help families slow down and share stories. She is the author of *Onederland: A Mother's Story of Finding Hope in Hard Places* and *Begin*. Find her @elizabethmaxon or elizabethmaxon.com.

Shelly Miller is a veteran ministry leader and sought-after mentor on Sabbath keeping. She leads the Sabbath Society, an online community of people who want to make rest a rhythm of life, and her writing has been featured in several national publications. She is the author of *Rhythms of Rest: Finding the Spirit of Sabbath in a Busy World*. Visit Shelly's blog, Redemption's Beauty, at www.redemptionsbeauty.com, for stories about the adventure of living as an expat in London. She is a vicar's wife and mother of two children.

Lynn D. Morrissey is author of *Love Letters to God: Deeper Intimacy Through Written Prayer* and other books, contributor to numerous bestsellers, Consilium and Deeper Waters blogger, speaker, and soloist. A professional journal facilitator (CJF), Lynn is passionate about encouraging transparency in women through her ministry, Sacred Journaling. She and Michael have been married since 1975 and have one beautiful grown daughter, Sheridan. Contact Lynn at words@brick.net or on Facebook.

Katie Kenny Phillips and her husband are raising their five children (three biological and two by way of foster care and adoption) in Atlanta, Georgia. She writes about the glory of when God shows up in the midst of a messy, hilarious, beautiful, obedient life at www.operationleapoffaith.com.

Wynter Pitts is the mother of four girls: Alena, Kaitlyn, Camryn, and Olivia. She is an author and the founder of For Girls Like You, a resource ministry for girls and their parents. Her oldest daughter, Alena, starred in the box office hit *War Room* (2015).

Elisa Pulliam is a life coach, author, and speaker, plus a wife and mom, and is passionate about inspiring women to embrace authentic life transformation through an encounter with God for the sake of impacting the next generation. Learn more at elisapulliam.com.

Christie Purifoy earned a PhD in English literature at the University of Chicago before trading the classroom for an old farmhouse and a garden. She lives in Pennsylvania with her husband and four children, where she observes the seasonal beauty of God's good creation. Her first book is *Roots and Sky: A Journey Home in Four Seasons.*

Anna Rendell is the social media coordinator at incourage.me, the author of *A Moment of Christmas: Daily Devotions for Time-Strapped Moms,* and shares from her heart at GirlWithBlog.com. Anna and her husband, Jared, live in Minnesota with their three kids, who provide plenty of fodder for her weekly #realmomconfessions on Facebook. She loves a good book and a great latte.

Rachel Anne Ridge is an artist and writer, mom to three grown kids, and Nana to two littles. She blogs daily humor and encouragement at www.HomeSanctuary.com. Her first book, *Flash, The Homeless Donkey Who Taught Me About Life, Faith and Second Chances,* released in May 2015 by Tyndale.

Deidra Riggs is a leader, speaker, and author who works to build bridges and tear down the walls that divide us—in our culture, our neighborhoods, our hearts, and the church. Deidra is the author of *Every Little Thing: Making a World of Difference Right Where You Are* and *ONE: Unity in a Divided World.* Sign up for her newsletter at deidrariggs.com.

Danielle Smith is an author, speaker, host, and mom to two amazing small people. She shares regular encouragement for moms seeking their own version of "good enough" at www.PrettyExtraordinary.com. Her first book was *Mom, Incorporated: A Guide to Business and Baby.*

Wendy Speake is a trained actress and heartfelt Bible teacher who is passionate about pointing women to Christ. She's the coauthor of the popular parenting book *Triggers* and *Life Creative*. For more stories that inspire love and faith, follow along at wendyspeake.com.

Rachel Macy Stafford is the *New York Times* bestselling author of *Hands Free Mama, Hands Free Life,* and *Only Love Today*. Rachel inspires people to choose love as much as humanly possible through her blog, handsfreemama.com, and through speaking events. Rachel relishes life in the South with her husband, two daughters, and two rescue cats.

Kelli Stuart is a storyteller, a wife, a mom, and the driver of a smokin' hot minivan. She lives in Tampa, Florida, with her husband and four children. Kelli is the author of the acclaimed historical fiction novel *Like a River from Its Course*, and the coauthor of *Life Creative: Inspiration for Today's Renaissance Mom*, both with Kregel Publications. Find out more at www.kellistuart.com.

Teri Lynne Underwood is a pastor's wife, ministry speaker, and Bible teacher. As the founder of www.PrayersforGirls.com, Teri Lynne is a cheerleader for girls' moms and the author of *Praying for Girls: Asking God for the Things They Need Most* (Bethany House, 2017).

Amanda White is a wife, mama to two, and God-lover. She blogs creative parenting ideas at ohAmanda.com. Her family devotional, *Truth in the Tinsel: An Advent Experience for Little Hands*, has been enjoyed by tens of thousands of families.

Adrian H. Wood, PhD, is a rural Eastern NC mother of four, one with extra special needs. She offers personal glimpses where satire meets truth, faith meets irony, and despair meets joy. This educated debutante escapes the laundry and finds true meaning in graceful transparency.

KariAnne Wood is an author and blogger and a mom to two boys and two girls. She blogs all things decorating and DIY tips sprinkled with inspiration at thistlewoodfarms.com. Her first book, *So Close to Amazing*, was released in September 2017 with Tyndale Publishing.